THE BALANCE OF PAYMENTS IN A
MONETARY ECONOMY

JOHN F. KYLE

The Balance of Payments in a Monetary Economy

PRINCETON UNIVERSITY PRESS

PRINCETON, NEW JERSEY

Copyright © 1976 by Princeton University Press
PUBLISHED BY PRINCETON UNIVERSITY PRESS, PRINCETON, NEW JERSEY
IN THE UNITED KINGDOM: PRINCETON UNIVERSITY PRESS, GUILDFORD,
SURREY
ALL RIGHTS RESERVED
Library of Congress Cataloging in Publication data will
be found on the last printed page of this book
This book has been composed in
'Monophoto' Times Mathematics, Series 569B
PRINTED IN THE UNITED STATES OF AMERICA
BY PRINCETON UNIVERSITY PRESS,
PRINCETON, NEW JERSEY

To Claire

Introduction to the Fourth Winner
of the Irving Fisher Award

THIS is the fourth volume in the series of Irving Fisher Award Monographs, sponsored by Omicron Delta Epsilon, The International Honor Society in Economics. The author of this volume, Professor John F. Kyle of New York University, is the winner of the 1973 Irving Fisher Award. There was no award in 1972; the Final Selection Board decided that none of the entries met the high standards established for this prestigious award. 1973, on the other hand, was a banner year with five finalists selected by the International Editorial Board. Dr. Kyle's entry, submitted by the University of Wisconsin (which also submitted the entry of the second winner of the award, Charles R. Nelson), was adjudged the best of the five and worthy of the award by the Final Selection Board consisting of Professors William J. Baumol, Frank H. Hahn, Leonid Hurwicz, Wassily Leontief, and Egon Neuberger (ex officio). I am grateful to the members of the International Editorial Board and Final Selection Board who devoted some of their scarcest resource, time, to making the Irving Fisher Award Series the important contribution that it has become in the encouragement of quality of scholarship by the entering members of our profession.

I wish to thank Professor Richard Dusansky, the Associate Editor, and the members of the International Executive Board of Omicron Delta Epsilon, particularly Professors Sylvia Lane, Alan A. Brown, and Ervin K. Zingler. Without their cooperation the series would not have been possible.

Egon Neuberger
EDITOR

PREFACE

THIS study is a revised and extended version of my Ph.D. dissertation, which was written at the University of Wisconsin under the supervision of Professor Robert E. Baldwin. I am deeply indebted to him and to the other members of my dissertation committee, Professors J. David Richardson and Kenneth R. Smith, for their numerous helpful comments and generous contributions of time to that project. I am also indebted to my former colleague and sometime coauthor, Jon Harkness, now of McMaster University, for helpful comments on various portions of that earlier manuscript. In addition, I would like to thank the members of the Irving Fisher Award Selection Board, Professors William J. Baumol, Frank H. Hahn, Leonid Hurwicz, Wassily Leontief, and Egon Neuberger, for their encouraging comments in connection with their selection of my dissertation for the 1973 Irving Fisher Award.

For help in converting the original dissertation into the present monograph, I am especially indebted to Professor Peter B. Kenan for his helpful comments and assistance. In addition to numerous suggestions that have materially improved the organization and exposition of the entire study, I am indebted to him for pointing out that there was a direct connection between some of my results and others found in the monetarist literature, and for suggesting the analysis found in section I of Chapter 4.

Most of all, I am indebted to my wife, Claire, who, in addition to putting in long hours as graphic artist, typist, and proofreader, also undertook the laborious task of rechecking all mathematical derivations, thereby saving me from several embarrassing mistakes. As if this were not enough, she also managed to put up with a sometimes irritable, often inaccessible husband, all that I might finish the vanity of this study.

With assistance like this, there can be no doubt that I alone am responsible for any errors that remain.

JFK

New York, New York
May 1975

TABLE OF CONTENTS

TABLE OF CONTENTS

THE BALANCE OF PAYMENTS IN A
MONETARY ECONOMY

CHAPTER 1

Approaches to the Analysis of Devaluation: A Brief Survey

DESPITE several significant advances in recent years, it remains true that the monetary aspects of international economic theory are much less fully understood than are its barter properties, and the conclusions of most monetary analyses are much less definitive. Perhaps the best illustration of this is the fact that the unsuspecting reader, first approaching the balance of payments adjustment literature, can readily find three distinct, unreconciled approaches to the analysis of the impact of exchange rate changes on the balance of payments. Since none of the three approaches[1] has discredited or disproved the other two, the need for a reconciliation, or synthesis, of the various approaches is readily apparent.

One excellent question that might be asked by the reader upon discovering that this somewhat surprising state of affairs has prevailed for some time is how it could have arisen in the first place. Fortunately, this question has a ready answer. As Anne Krueger noted in her now classic survey (Krueger 1969), the decade-long debate over the relative merits of the relative price and income approaches to devaluation analysis[2]

[1] Briefly, the three are (1) the relative price (elasticities) approach, (2) the income (absorption) approach, and (3) the portfolio-balance (monetarist) approach.

[2] The debate can be properly said to have begun when Alexander published a paper attacking the traditional relative price approach to devaluation analysis, and setting forth his own absorption approach as an alternative (Alexander 1952). It continued through Machlup's criticisms of Alexander (Machlup 1955, 1956), and Alexander's attempted reconciliation (Alexander 1959), and culminated in Tsiang's 1961 attempt at synthesis. Along the way, numerous other authors contributed commentary, extensions, and attempts at synthesis, the most significant of which are discussed below.

3

resulted, not in a satisfactory synthesis of the two approaches, but rather in the rediscovery of the significance of monetary factors in sustaining a balance of payments disequilibrium.[3] This rediscovery, in turn, has given rise to the monetarist approach, in which relative price and income changes are ignored or assumed away in order to focus exclusively on the role of money in the adjustment process.

According to Krueger (1969), the failure to reconcile successfully the relative price and income (elasticities and absorption) approaches resulted from the lack of an analytical model sufficiently general to incorporate both relative price and monetary phenomena and yet specific enough to generate results useful to the policy maker. With the recent rise of the monetarist approach, this statement easily can be said to characterize the reason for the lack of a thorough integration of this approach with the other two as well.

In this study, a model capable of integrating all three approaches to devaluation analysis is developed and explained. One of the basic contentions of this monograph, supported by results presented in later chapters, is that to integrate fully the relative price, income, and monetarist approaches it is necessary to construct a model that explicitly includes (a) a production sector, (b) a complete monetary sector, and (c) a carefully developed demand sector, all of which permit the simultaneous interaction of changing prices and incomes. To date, no model containing all of these elements has been employed in international economic theory. Furthermore, many of the existing models built along macroeconomic lines are misspecified in that they fail to take account of the fact that, in an open economy, real output and real income in general are not equal.

These flaws in currently used macroeconomic models have

---

[3] A similar conclusion was reached by Tsiang (1961).

several additional effects aside from preventing a complete integration of the various approaches to devaluation analysis. For one thing, in order for the models to be internally consistent, it tends to be necessary to assume that domestic prices in all countries are fixed, with only exchange rate changes allowed. This, in turn, implies that terms-of-trade effects are generally absent from the analysis.[4] Furthermore, the structure of existing models means that the "full employment" case must be handled in a rather unsatisfactory way. Currently it is simply assumed that at full employment output of all goods is fixed, which can be shown to be inconsistent with the standard Classical labor market assumptions.[5]

Rather than take a macroeconomic approach, a number of authors have adapted Walrasian general equilibrium models to allow for money, and have analyzed the problem in this framework. To some extent these models do not contain as many problems as the more traditional macroeconomic ones, and they have the virtue of relating directly to the barter models. On the other hand, they suffer because of the rather restrictive nature of the Walrasian system itself. Full employment, fixed factor supplies, instant malleability of capital, and no real financial sector (i.e. no alternative asset to money) all tend to make the world they describe something less than perfectly general. In addition, it is difficult at times to see how the worlds described by the macroeconomic (especially the Keynesian) and Walrasian systems relate to one another.

In the remaining chapters of this study, analysis of the financial aspects of international economic theory takes two steps forward and one step backward. The steps forward result from the removal of many of the limitations in existing

---

[4] Tsiang is an exception here, but his lack of an explicit production sector limits his analysis. Furthermore, it is not clear just how his terms-of-trade effect fits into the general model he discusses.

[5] See Chapter 3.

5

analyses. Thus, Chapter 2 presents a formal analysis of the specification errors commonly found in earlier, open-economy aggregate models. Chapter 3 gives a macroeconomic analysis of the short-run aspects of the balance of payments in a monetary economy, which avoids the specification pitfalls discussed in Chapter 2 and which provides for a complete integration of the elasticities and absorption approaches to devaluation analysis. This analysis, which initially is conducted in a Keynesian, less than full-employment framework, also is modified to allow for a Classical labor supply function.

Since the results obtained in Chapter 3 depend on an assumption that the payments surplus or deficit is completely sterilized by the monetary authorities, Chapter 4 extends the model by relaxing this assumption. Since relaxation of the sterilization assumption is shown to require the development of a long-run model, Chapter 4 also presents a comparison of the results obtained in the "monetary" model developed in Chapter 3 with those found in the monetarist literature. In this comparison, many of the results found in the monetarist literature are shown to be special cases of the model developed in this study. This chapter also discusses the effects of monetary and fiscal policy in a properly specified open-economy model.

In Chapter 5, the basic results of the macroeconomic analysis of Chapters 3 and 4 are related to conclusions derived in the modified Walrasian setting employed by some monetarist-school writers to examine the role of nontraded goods in the adjustment process. In addition to the comparison, these Walrasian-type models with both money and nontraded goods are extended to allow for an alternative financial asset (bonds) and a rate of interest in one case, and a variable labor supply and unemployment in another. Chapter 6 is a conclusion.

The analysis outlined above constitutes the steps forward. At the same time, a step backward is taken in that the focus of the analysis is the trade account of the balance of payments.

In recent years, especially with the rise of the monetarist approach to payments analysis, much attention has been devoted to the capital account, and away from the current account. Because of its complexities, however, the integrated model developed in the following chapters examines only the current account aspects of the balance of payments. While clearly a limitation, this restricted focus permits a clearer exposition and development of the main new features of the model than otherwise would be practical. However, it is a limitation that should be removed by future research as soon as possible.

Before the analysis outlined above is undertaken, however, the rest of this chapter is devoted to a survey of the existing approaches to payments analysis.[6]

I THE TRADITIONAL ELASTICITIES ANALYSIS

Devaluation has long been the "policy of last resort" for countries suffering from a persistent deficit in their balance of trade. This is simply another way of saying that a general assumption of policy makers has been that an increase in the domestic price of foreign currencies will make foreign goods more expensive to domestic residents and domestic goods cheaper to foreign residents, thus reducing imports and increasing exports. However, even under conditions of perfect competition, it is well-known that devaluation may result in a deterioration in the current account balance rather than in its improvement. Quite reasonably, therefore, the question early was asked as to the conditions under which the trade balance would improve following a change in the exchange rate.

---

[6] Two excellent, albeit somewhat dated, comprehensive surveys of the earlier portion of this literature are Krueger (1969) and Clement, Pfister, and Rothwell (1967, Chapter 7).

Derivation via the Balance of Payments Equation

Until the widespread acceptance of Keynesian income analysis, the answer to this question was generally believed to have been given by the celebrated "four elasticities" formula,[7] and its special case, the Marshall-Lerner condition. The formula is generally derived by defining the balance of trade as the difference between the value of exports and the value of imports, both measured either in units of the domestic or the foreign currency, then differentiating this expression with respect to the exchange rate. The object of this exercise is to obtain the conditions under which the trade balance improves with a devaluation. The expression that emerges is referred to as the "four elasticities" formula because it was initially believed that these conditions could be expressed entirely in terms of the (partial equilibrium) elasticities of demand and supply for exports and imports.

The exact derivation of the elasticities condition varies from article to article, but the result is essentially the same. One such derivation yields[8]

$$(1.1) \qquad \frac{dB}{de} = -\left\{ X\left[\frac{\sigma_X(1 + \eta_X)}{\sigma_X - \eta_X} \right] + F\left[\frac{\eta_F(\sigma_F + 1)}{\sigma_F - \eta_F} \right] \right\},$$

where dB = the change in the home country's trade balance, measured in units of the domestic currency,

de = the change in the exchange rate,

X and F = the value of exports and imports, respectively (both measured in units of the domestic currency),

σ_i and η_i = the elasticities of supply and demand, respec-

---

[7] The standard references here seem to be Robinson (1937), and Metzler (1948).

[8] This particular derivation can be found in Alexander (1959). Notation has been changed to be consistent with the model developed in subsequent chapters of this study.

tively, for the ith good, $i = X,F$. (Demand elasticities are defined negatively.)

Since what is of interest are the conditions under which $dB/de > 0$, it is clear that definite results depend on the magnitude of the σ_i and η_i. One famous result is obtained by assuming that trade is balanced, initially, so that $X = F$, then assuming that the $\sigma_i \to \infty$. In this case equation (1.1) reduces to

$$(1.2) \qquad \frac{dB}{de} = -X(1 + \eta_X + \eta_F).$$

Equation (1.2) immediately yields the well-known Marshall-Lerner condition (i.e. that $dB/de > 0$ if $|\eta_X + \eta_F| > 1$).

Foreign Exchange Market Stability Condition

Essentially the same results can be obtained by a slightly different route, namely as a stability condition of the foreign exchange market. By looking at the supply of and demand for foreign exchange as functions of the exchange rate, one can require that the market be stable, which implies that an increase (decrease) in the price of foreign exchange (i.e. devaluation (revaluation)) leads to a reduction (increase) in the excess demand. The assumption of a stable foreign market, in turn, requires that the elasticity of supply of foreign exchange exceed the elasticity of demand in absolute value. By assuming that only current account transactions take place, one can relate the elasticities of the foreign exchange supply and demand curves directly to the elasticities of the supply and demand curves for exports and imports. From this and an assumption of initially balanced trade it follows that $dB/de > 0$ if

$$(1.3) \qquad 1 + \eta_X + \eta_F < \frac{\eta_X \eta_F}{\sigma_X \sigma_F}(1 + \sigma_X + \sigma_F).$$

This also reduces to the Marshall-Lerner condition as the $\sigma_i \to \infty$.[9]

Objections

There are several well-known and valid theoretical objections to the traditional elasticities model. These may be summarized by noting that, regardless of the approach, the analysis is essentially a partial equilibrium one. That is, what was intended by the various authors was that the supply and demand elasticities presented in the formulae given above be those of standard microeconomic theory. For this to be true, it must be assumed that incomes and prices of all other goods remain constant,[10] which is clearly unrealistic. Even if governmental authorities take explicit steps to hold incomes constant, it is highly unlikely that prices of other commodities will remain unchanged after the devaluation.[11]

II THE "REVISED TRADITIONAL" ANALYSIS AND ABSORPTION

"Revised Traditional" Models

Recognition of the limitations in the tradition models led to several attempts to amend the analysis to include the possibility of income and/or price changes. One ingenious "out"

[9] See Vanek (1962) for a complete discussion of this approach. The fact that there was such a relationship between the two approaches first seems to have been mentioned explicitly by Machlup (1955).

[10] In some models an assumption of zero cross-price effect is sufficient to obtain the result in a general equilibrium context. See section IV below. This is clearly a very restrictive assumption, however.

[11] Note that an assumption of full employment will not solve anything here. In this case, a devaluation will lead to a movement along a transformation surface, which clearly causes prices of all goods to change. Furthermore, as will be shown later, devaluation will change the level of income even if "full employment" is constantly maintained. In a Keynesian unemployment situation it is clearly unreasonable to assume that the authorities will attempt to keep income levels constant.

was the attempt by Sohmen (1957) and others to redefine the elasticities computed above as "total" rather than partial ones. That is, "the price elasticities . . . were to be computed as if all adjustments caused by devaluation had been permitted to have their ultimate influence on the price-quantity relationship for the internationally traded goods" (Clement, Pfister, and Rothwell 1967, p. 287). Unfortunately, while theoretically valid, this approach is useless as a guide to policy makers since the computation of such total elasticities clearly borders on the impossible.

In the early 1950s, in response to an earlier suggestion of Tinbergen (1941), a series of papers emerged presenting an alternate approach that Clement, Pfister, and Rothwell (1967) have referred to as the "revised traditional variant." These models, which were clearly Keynesian in motivation, provided for the possibility of secondary price and income changes in the rest of the economy as well as allowing for the types of adjustments described by the four elasticities approach. Although not as completely worked out as many of the elasticities-absorption synthesis models to be discussed below, the revised traditional variants were of essentially the same form. That is, they treated the elasticities result as the initial, or, primary, effect of the devaluation, which then led to secondary income effects that might either reinforce (unusual) or offset (to be expected) part of the initial effect.

As has been pointed out elsewhere, this

> reformulation of the traditional elasticities approach, incorporating as it did either income elasticities or marginal or average propensities to import and save, gave rise to even more complex stability condition formulas. . . . Nevertheless, a major advantage of this approach, in comparison with both the *ceteris paribus* and "total" elasticities formulations, was that in explicitly recognizing that devaluation has significant effects beyond merely altering the exchange rate,

11

and hence relative export and import prices, attention is directed to the roles of income effects in the devaluation mechanism (Clement, Pfister, and Rothwell 1967, p. 288).

However, this positive effect was felt to be somewhat "offset" by the fact that these models reinforced some of the earlier "elasticities pessimism," which held that it was unlikely that the sum of the demand elasticities would exceed unity, by making the conditions for an effective devaluation even more stringent.[12]

Typical of these results is that of Harberger (1950).[13] In his "Keynesian Model," where variation in output and national income is allowed, Harberger derives an expression for the change in the trade balance following a devaluation as

$$(1.4) \qquad \frac{dB}{de} = -\frac{hh^*X(1 + \eta_X + \eta_F + f + f^*)}{hh^* + fh^* + f^*h},$$

where B = balance of trade,

h, h^* = marginal propensity to hoard in the home and foreign country, respectively,

η_X, η_F = elasticity of demand for exports and imports in the home country,

f, f^* = marginal propensity to import in the home and foreign country, respectively,

X = exports of the home country, and

e = exchange rate.

Since h, h^*, f, f^*, and X are all positive, it is clear that the

---

[12] It is never made clear in all these discussions in the literature why the benefits from the derivation of a more accurate result are somehow partially "offset" because the results indicate that the world is more complex than previously believed. The terminology is retained here because it seems to be common in the literature, but it should be remembered that the value judgments implied do not mean much.

[13] Similar results have been obtained by Johnson (1956), and Laursen and Metzler (1950) among others.

necessary condition for a devaluation to be successful is that the absolute value of the sum of the η exceed unity plus the sum of the f, i.e. that $|\eta_X + \eta_F| > 1 + f + f^*$.[14]

The response to results such as Harberger's seemed to be that they greatly complicated the analysis and made it much harder to estimate empirically the relevant parameters. In addition, many authors did not believe that available empirical evidence supported the implication of Harberger's results that it would be difficult for a devaluation to improve the trade balance. To avoid many of the difficulties inherent in the revised traditional variant, both theoretical and empirical, Alexander (1952) tried a completely new tack, emphasizing the macroeconomic aspects of the problem.

Absorption

Alexander's absorption approach represents an extremely straightforward application to an open economy of the standard Keynesian closed economy model. As is well known, Keynesian theory has an identity relationship between aggregate supply and aggregate demand, which, for a open economy, can be expressed as

$$\text{Aggregate Supply} \qquad \text{Aggregate Demand}$$

$$(1.5) \qquad Y \qquad \equiv C + I + G + (X - F)$$

where, as usual, $Y =$ value of aggregate output,

$C =$ value of aggregate consumption expenditure,

$I =$ value of aggregate investment expenditure,

$G =$ value of aggregate government expenditure,

$X =$ value of exports,

$F =$ value of imports,

---

[14] Equation (1.4) holds under the assumptions of infinitely elastic supply curves and initially balanced trade. It should be noted that Harberger also derives a more general result which relaxes the latter assumption.

and all variables are measured in real terms. Note that the balance of trade, B, is equal to the difference between exports and imports, so that $B \equiv X - F$, and call the sum of $C + I + G$ national expenditure, or absorption (A). Then equation (1.5) can be rewritten as

(1.6) $B \equiv Y - A$,

which emphasizes a rather basic point, namely that any trade deficit arises because current national expenditure, or absorption, exceeds national output. To understand the effect a devaluation has on the balance of trade, in this context, involves determining its effects on the relative levels of national output and national expenditure. As Johnson (1958) has pointed out, an important contribution of this approach is "the light [it] sheds on the policy problem of correcting a deficit by relating the balance of payments to the overall operation of the economy rather than treating it as one sector of the economy to be analysed by itself" (p. 158).

Alexander's analysis is based entirely on equation (1.6). By taking the change in equation (1.6),

(1.7) $\Delta B = \Delta Y - \Delta A$,

or, letting lower-case letters represent changes in upper-case variables,

(1.8) $b = y - a$.

Alexander then goes on to argue that changes in A can be divided into two components: (1) changes that are induced via changes in income (indirect effects), and (2) changes that are a direct result of the devaluation. Let c be the marginal propensity to spend out of a change in income, and denote the direct effect on absorption by d. Then $a = cy + d$, and equation (1.8) becomes

(1.9) $b = (1 - c)y - d$.

According to Alexander, the formulation of the problem suggested by equation (1.9) leads to three basic questions:

(a) How does the devaluation affect income?
(b) How does a change in the level of income affect absorption, i.e. how large is c?
(c) How does the devaluation directly affect absorption at any given level of income, i.e. how large is d?

The answer to (b) is, conceptually at least, quite straightforward. As long as c is less than unity, any increase in income will increase absorption by less than the increase in income, and thus the trade balance will improve. If c is greater than or equal to unity, then the trade balance will improve only if the direct effects of the devaluation exceed the induced effects.

In his 1952 paper, rather than attempt a precise statement of the various relationships in his model, Alexander merely summarized the main effects he felt would take place. These are divided into income effects and direct effects. Income effects are: (i) the idle resource effect, normally positive, and (ii) the terms of trade effect, normally negative. Under direct effects are found (i) the cash balance effect (positive), (ii) an income redistribution effect (unclear), (iii) a money illusion effect (also unclear), and (iv) various miscellaneous effects. (See Alexander 1952, pp. 267–274, for a full statement.)

III MACHLUP'S ATTACK AND SOME ATTEMPTS AT SYNTHESIS

Absorption Criticized

In two strongly worded papers, Machlup (1955, 1956) sharply criticized the absorption analysis discussed above. While admitting that the traditional elasticities approach was deficient in several dimensions, Machlup attacked Alexander's article as being more misleading than helpful. His criticisms were based on several points. Alexander had argued that the traditional elasticities approach was tautological. Machlup threw the same charge back at him. According to Machlup, Alexander's fundamental equation (equation (1.5) above) was nothing more than a definition, and therefore his absorption analysis was nothing more than implicit theorizing based on tautologies. Furthermore, this implicit theorizing, Machlup said, missed an essential point of a devaluation study. In Alexander's paper, all quantities are real variables, while from a balance of payments standpoint what ought to be considered are money values. Since it is clearly possible for the "real" and money balances to move in opposite directions,[15] an analysis based on real values may well be misleading from a policy maker's point of view.

Machlup further criticized Alexander for his neglect of relative price effects. As Clement, Pfister, and Rothwell point out (1967, p. 293), one of Alexander's contributions lies in using the absorption model to examine the effects of devaluation under the differing cases of full employment and unemployment. Even in Alexander's analysis, the two cases are characterized by differing supply and demand conditions in the commodity markets, i.e. they depend on elasticities. Furthermore, the magnitude of the impact of his direct effects also depends on assumptions about various elasticities.

---

[15] By definition, the money balance of trade is the value of exports less the value of imports, while the real balance is the money balance divided by the appropriate price index. Let X and F be the quantities of exports and imports, respectively, and p and eq their prices in units of the domestic currency (i.e. eq = foreign price $\times$ exchange rate). Also, let Φ be the price index = $\alpha p + (1 - \alpha)eq$. If initially $p = eq = 1$, and $X = 100, F = 200$, then $B_{real} = B_{money} = 100 - 200 = -100$. Now assume that X rises to 120, F falls to 115, but eq rises to 2 (let $\alpha = .8$). Then $B_{real} \simeq -92$, while $B_{money} = -110$, and the "real" balance has improved while the money balance has deteriorated.

Alexander's Synthesis

Without explicitly admitting that he was responding to Machlup's criticisms, in 1959 Alexander produced a second paper that attempted to combine the elasticities and absorption approaches. In this analysis, which was presented in a much more mathematically rigorous fashion than his first paper, he set out a model that treated the traditional elasticities effects, based on assumptions of constant money incomes, as the impact effects of a devaluation. These impact effects, he argued, then caused changes in money income that also affected the trade balance via secondary "reversal" effects. In Alexander's view, the absorption analysis he had worked out earlier provided the framework within which these reversal factors could be examined.

Without going into the details of his derivations (Alexander 1959, appendix), Alexander's basic results can be presented readily. Define a reversal factor, R, as the effects of a change in income, brought about by the initial elasticities effect, on the trade balance. In a two-country analysis, there are two such effects, R and R^*, one for each country. Alexander argued that, in general $0 < R, R^* < 1$. Let $E =$ right-hand side of equation (1.1). Then, in the final Alexander synthesis,

$$(1.10) \qquad \frac{dB}{de} = \frac{RR^*E}{1 - (R - 1)(R^* - 1)}.$$

The multiplier $RR^*/[1 - (R - 1)(R^* - 1)]$ is the final reversal factor. The product RR^* is the initial reversal, and the term $1/[1 - (R - 1)(R^* - 1)]$ gives the sum of an infinite series of adjustments and readjustments of the initial reversals.

Equation (1.10) can be reworked to include marginal propensities to spend on imports and marginal propensities to hoard, both defined with respect to money income. Let h and f be, respectively, the marginal propensities to hoard and import,

17

and define $H = h/(h + f)$ and $Z = f/(h + f)$. Similar asterisked expressions hold for the foreign country.

Alexander argues that, if the initial effect of a devaluaion is measured in units of the domestic currency and if initially the entire change in the trade balance is an increase in expenditure in the home country, then (money) income rises by $E/(h + f)$, so that the trade balance deteriorates by $f[E/(h + f)] = ZE$. Thus, after the initial reaction by the devaluing country, the trade balance is $E - ZE = E(1 - Z) = HE$. But, by definition, this equals RE, so $H = R$ and $Z = 1 - R$ and likewise for H^* and Z^*. Using these results, equation (1.10) reduces to

$$(1.11) \qquad \frac{dB}{de} = \frac{HH^*E}{1 - ZZ^*}.$$

Furthermore, by defining $v = f/h$, and likewise for v^*, then $H = 1/(v + 1)$ and $Z = v/(v + 1)$. From this, it is apparent that equation (1.11) reduces to

$$(1.12) \qquad \frac{dB}{de} = \frac{E}{1 + v + v^*},$$

which is the final synthesis formula. From equation (1.12), it can be seen that the reversal factors depend only on the ratios of the money-income-induced factors. The larger are the f relative to the h, the greater will be the final reversal effect, and the smaller will be the final effect of a devaluation. Although he relaxes some of his restrictive assumption later (e.g. the assumption of an initial $B = 0$), Alexander clearly regards equation (1.12) as his fundamental result.

The "synthesis" presented in equation (1.12) has been severely criticized by Tsiang (1961) as being no synthesis at all. As Tsiang points out, the idea of using a two-stage analysis to incorporate both elasticity and income effects was essentially what had been done before the Alexander-Machlup debate, so

18

that, on this count at least, nothing new had been added. Indeed, Alexander himself admitted that equation (1.12) was "essentially a simplification and generalization of results first obtained by Harberger (1950, eq. 14)" (Alexander 1959, p.31).[16] However Tsiang does not say that Alexander contributed nothing to devaluation analysis. Quite to the contrary, in fact, he argues that, although a complete answer was not provided, useful insights were gained and he offered his own synthesis based on these insights. Before examining Tsiang's contribution, however, it is useful to discuss briefly some other attempts at synthesis.

Synthesis a la Brems and Michaely

Alexander's attempt at a synthesis came in 1959. The honor for the first such attempt to meet Machlup's criticisms, however, seems to belong to Hans Brems. In a paper in the *Economic Journal* (Brems 1957), he presented a Leontief fixed-coefficients model of an underemployed open economy, which he used to analyze the devaluation question. In his model, Brems divided the economy into three sectors; firms, households, and government, and carefully distinguished between money and real income. Attention is also paid to the difference between ex ante and ex post behavior. The model, in which each country produces only one good, consists of 38 equations in as many unknowns describing some ten transactions, two of which are intrasectoral and eight intersectoral.

Since the model is highly restrictive by virtue of its fixed-coefficients technology, Cobb-Douglas demand curves, and the like, it does not seem worthwhile to reproduce any of Brem's rather elaborate results here. His principal conclusion on the efficiency of a devaluation seems to be that it will be

---

[16] The essential similarity between Alexander's and Harberger's results can be seen by multiplying the numerator and denominator of equation (1.4) by $1/hh^*$, and noting that f/h and f^*/h^* are Alexander's v and v^*, respectively.

successful, given his assumptions, if the income effect of a price change is large relative to the substitution effect, and unsuccessful if the converse holds. This result was accepted by Alexander as compatible with the conclusions of his model as well (Alexander 1959, p. 31).

Another attempt at reconciling the elasticities and absorption analyses came in a short but significant note by Michaely in 1960. While this paper came after Alexander's 1959 contribution, it just preceded Tsiang's important 1961 article, and was clearly a stimulus to Tsiang's work. Michaely noted that integration of the two approaches was not a problem under conditions of extensive unemployment, since both sides conceded that as long as there was a possibility for employment and output in the devaluing country to increase the trade balance ought to improve. Since the differences of opinion arise in the case of full employment, he limited himself to a discussion of that case.

The essential point of Michaely's paper is that whenever the same set of basic assumptions are made then the same conclusions logically must follow, regardless of the analytical method adopted. In particular, since the elasticities and absorption analyses seem to start from the same basic point, then they must yield the same results. The elasticities approach implies that a devaluation generates a change in the relative prices of export and import goods, and domestic goods. Profit maximization then requires a change in the relative quantities of these goods produced, which changes the trade balance. The absorption approach requires that absorption fall (income is held fixed in Michaely's full-employment world) if the devaluation is to be successful. Since both arguments are logically correct—one out of the assumption of profit maximization and one by definition—it must be shown either that if devaluation increases the prices of imports and exports relative to domestic prices it must cut absorption as well, or that if devaluation does

20

not cut absorption it cannot result in an increase in the relative prices of exports and imports.

Since Michaely's analysis is strictly verbal, no formulae or graphs can be presented to demonstrate his argument. However, the key to the reconciliation, in his view, is the cash-balance effect. The change in relative prices brought on by the devaluation leads to a reduction in real cash balances and, therefore, a reduction in absorption. This conclusion, in turn, leads Michaely to some observations about the role of money and various monetary policies in devaluation analysis. In particular, he states (without proof) that Keynesian neutral monetary policy (i.e. fixing the interest rate) will nullify the effect of a devaluation, while "orthodox neutral" monetary policy (i.e. fixing the nominal money supply) will make it a success.

While Michaely's analysis contained the seeds of Tsiang's important paper, he was unfortunately incorrect in his main conclusion. It is quite possible, once a model is properly specified, to integrate the elasticities and absorption approaches without appealing to the cash-balance effect. In particular, the integration presented in Chapter 3 of this study does not rely on a cash-balance effect to obtain any results. However, Michaely did correctly identify the importance of specifying the type of monetary policy (i.e. Keynesian neutral or orthodox neutral) being followed, given his assumption that the economy was at full employment. Furthermore, Tsiang's rather harsh criticisms notwithstanding, Michaely's emphasis on the monetary aspects of the problem clearly motivated much of Tsiang's (and other) later work.

The Role of Money: Tsiang's Synthesis

Tsiang's paper appeared in 1961. In it he notes the Alexander-Machlup controversy, the contributions of Brems, Michaely, and others, then asks what has been gained by the debate. In Tsiang's opinion, Alexander's solution to the synthesis problem

21

was unsatisfactory on two grounds: (1) it merely got back to the point already reached by Harberger (1950) and others some nine or ten years earlier; and (2) the two-stage type analysis was unacceptable in itself. Clearly (2) is the more serious criticism of the two. In Tsiang's view, the two-stage framework was unsatisfactory because it required all supply curves to be infinitely elastic so that all prices in all countries (imports excepted) remain constant. Otherwise the multiplier effect will generate further price changes and further substitutions in consumption between domestic and foreign goods, thus adding more rounds to the cycle.

Tsiang does not say that the Alexander-Machlup dispute makes no contributions to the literature, however. After asking his question, he answers it by asserting that Alexander and Machlup have led to the rediscovery of the important role played by the supply of money in balance of payments analysis.[17] However, he goes on to say that, in spite of this highlighting of monetary factors, no formulae or mathematical models—including Alexander's—have yet fully incorporated monetary variables—a deficit his paper is designed to eliminate.

The model Tsiang proposes as the correct way to synthesize the two approaches is an eleven-equation version of one developed by Meade (1951). According to Tsiang, only Meade was careful enough always to include monetary variables in his model, and Tsiang's own paper is needed only because Meade unfortunately restricted his analysis to some special cases that, in effect, rule out the interesting influences of the money supply. After setting out this model, Tsiang states the conditions for a

---

[17] Johnson (1958) also concludes that this was the major contribution of the Alexander-Machlup controversy. Clement, Pfister, and Rothwell (1967) argue that there was also a raising of the level of analytical rigor in devaluation analysis. Given the Harberger (1950) and Meade (1951) contribution, however, it is hard to see how this position can be defended.

devaluation to be sucessful for a variety of cases: (1) internal balance assumed; (2) Keynesian neutral monetary policy; and (3) orthodox neutral monetary policy. In all these cases he presents the conditions with and without a terms of trade effect, although the conclusion for case (1) (Meade's case) is that changes in the terms of trade have no effect on the final results since they are exactly offset by monetary policies designed to keep the level of output, and hence employment, constant. Tsiang also argues that (a) Keynesian neutral monetary policy biases the economy toward instability (at full employment, Tsiang asserts, it guarantees instability), (b) orthodox neutral monetary policy does not have these problems, and (c) under both regimes, the terms of trade effect makes a difference, but its effect is not significant enough to warrant concern.

It does not seem worthwhile to reproduce any of Tsiang's rather intricate formulae here. Although his paper is a landmark in the literature, his conclusions are both mathematically complex and intuitively hard to explain. Furthermore, since Tsiang does not present any of his derivations, it is not clear how he has obtained his results.[18] Specifically, in many cases it appears that, rather than explicitly solve a complete model, he simply adds on a term or two to the final equation. For example, it is not at all clear what his "terms of trade effect" really means. Since he lacks a production sector in his model, it does not appear that domestic prices are being permitted to change. But nowhere is there a statement indicating how terms of trade effects fit into the model. In the model presented

---

[18] Exactly what Tsiang is doing in his so-called stability analysis of the Keynesian neutral monetary policy also is not clear. On the face of it, his statements about the necessary conditions for stability are incorrect, and without having his system of differential equations available, it is not possible to determine whether or not he is referring to some special case. However, although such a special case is *possible*, from the information Tsiang has provided one must conclude that his results are "not proven." See Chapter 3 for a fuller discussion of this point.

in Chapter 3 of this study, changes in the terms of trade are automatically incorporated.

In addition, Tsiang's major criticism of both the Alexander synthesis and of the Harberger analysis—that the two-stage synthesis itself was unacceptable—turns out to be incorrect. In the model developed in Chapter 3, it is possible to separate the effects of a devaluation into price effects and income effects.[19] In neither case is the assumption of infinitely elastic supply curves in both countries necessary.[20]

One very interesting and important feature of Tsiang's model, however, was borrowed from Meade. He explicitly accounted for the fact that money income, real income, and real output are, in an open economy different variables. This was done by carefully distinguishing between quantities of goods and their money value, and by noting explicitly that real income is money income divided by a price index. The price index, in turn, is a weighted average of the two prices in each country, where the weights are the value shares of the two goods in total expenditure.[21] Since failure to recognize this distinction leads to serious specification errors in other analyses, this correct feature of Tsiang's analysis deserves credit.

In spite of its serious limitations, Tsiang's paper deserves recognition as a major contribution to the literature. In it are the first rigorous demonstrations (aside from Meade's little-read work) of the importance of monetary variables, and the first suggestion of the proper way to handle real variables in an

---

[19] This separation property also was obtained by Richardson (1971) in a less general model.

[20] Tsiang's conclusions may stem from his apparent tendency to attack the problem by adding on effects to a simple initial equation rather than obtaining a general expression by solving a complete system of simultaneous equations.

[21] Tsiang's demand functions have total expenditure rather than income as an argument, along with the interest rate and relative prices, as do Meade's. Tsiang argues that this is an important advance made by Meade, but it is not clear that it merits the praise he gives it.

open economy model. In addition, along with the paper by Hahn discussed in the next section, it provided much of the impetus for the modern monetarist approach, as well as much of the motivation for this study.

IV WALRASIAN GENERAL EQUILIBRIUM, MONEY, AND NONTRADED GOODS

The Walrasian general equilibrium model has long been the standard framework within which most of the theorems in the real, or barter, theory of international trade have been derived. It is not surprising, therefore, that attempts have been made to introduce money into the model so as to analyze the balance of payments in this context as well. Since the framework of Walrasian analysis is, on the surface at least, rather different from the Keynesian general equilibrium world,[22] a comparison of the results obtained in the former with those already discussed above is of some interest.

General Equilibrium and Money

The first significant contribution in the Walrasian framework came from Hahn (1959). The model was the standard two-country, two-goods one, into which Hahn inserted two fiat currencies.[23] Before doing this, however, he demonstrated that in the model without money there were two alternative sufficiency conditions for the balance of payments to improve when the terms of trade deteriorate: (1) that the sum of the

---

[22] In the Walrasian system, factors of production are in fixed supply, instantly transferable between industries and always fully employed. Full employment is guaranteed, not by government policy, but rather by flexible prices and wages.

[23] As introduced by Hahn, money essentially is another commodity, the demand function for which is homogeneous of degree one in money income and prices, rather than degree zero.

marginal propensities to spend on imports (in terms of the numeraire) should exceed unity, and (2) that the two goods should be gross substitutes in the world market. When fiat currencies are introduced, the basic result is obtained: "Assuming the goods market to be in equilibrium both before and after a change in the rate of exchange, the balance of payments of country (1) will change in the same direction as the price of currency (2) in terms of currency (1) changes provided all goods and currencies are gross substitutes" (Hahn 1959, p. 117). As a special case, Hahn finds that if the devaluing country is small, so that its barter terms of trade cannot change, then devaluation necessarily improves the trade balance regardless of whether or not goods are gross substitutes.

Results identical to Hahn's later were produced by Kemp (1962). The only significant addition in Kemp's paper was the fact that the real-balance effect was shown to play an important role in the actual mechanics of the adjustment process. However, the same condition—that all goods and currencies be gross substitutes—emerges in Kemp's model. Likewise, he also finds that in the small-country case the balance of trade always improves with a devaluation, and that an assumption of zero cross-price elasticities for all goods is sufficient to generate the familiar four elasticities condition.

A second issue, namely the direction of movement of the terms of trade, turns out to be independent of the result on the balance of payments. That is, gross substitutability guarantees a successful devaluation regardless of whether the terms of trade improve or deteriorate. Improvement or deterioration, in turn depends on the relative size of ratios of marginal propensities to consume of the two countries. Specifically Hahn shows that $dt/de \gtreqless 0$ as $m_1/m_2 \lesseqgtr m^*_1/m^*_2$, where $t =$ terms of trade of the home country, $e =$ exchange rate, and m_i, $m_i^* =$ marginal propensity to consume good i in the home and foreign countries, respectively.

26

Introducing Nontraded Goods

One question of some interest to balance of payments theorists is the role nontraded goods play in the adjustment mechanism. The first serious investigation of the question seems to have been provided by Pearce (1961).[24] Although Pearce's model is neither of the Walrasian general equilibrium type nor monetary, mention of it is included here since it was obviously the stimulus to later papers. According to Pearce, a devaluation will cause the price of home goods to fall relative to traded goods, resulting in a shift in production away from home goods over to traded goods and conversely for consumption. In a fully employed economy, and with no change in output allowed, this clearly requires a cut in real expenditures. For a devaluation to be successful in improving the trade balance, therefore, the following are required (in order of importance):

1. A cut in money spending equal to
    a. the trade balance improvement, plus
    b. the money equivalent of the real gain or loss due to the change in the terms of trade (c.f. (3)) plus.
    c. the money equivalent of any change in tariff revenue due to the change in the terms of trade.
2. A fall in the price of nontraded goods relative to that of traded goods.
3. Some change in the real terms of trade which may be

[24] Kemp (1962) suggested another role for home goods by noting that the Robinson-Metzler four-elasticities formula could be made consistent with a general equilibrium analysis if it were assumed that there existed a class of nontraded goods comprising a large enough percentage of total spending that the income elasticity of demand for traded goods effectively was zero. Since it was shown that the four-elasticities formula is consistent with a general equilibrium analysis if it is assumed that all cross-price effects are zero (Negishi, 1968), Kemp's suggestion (hopefully not made with any degree of seriousness) was not adopted. (Kemp has adopted the Negishi assumption in his textbook; see Kemp 1969.)

27

positive or negative. *This will be small relative to change* (2).

As Krueger (1969) points out, in Pearce's model it is not clear how a devalution generates these required changes, especially (1). Two recent papers in the Hahn (1959) tradition have provided some answers to these questions. Kemp (1970) has shown that, if all commodities are weak gross substitutes (and all marginal propensities to consume are positive), then devaluation will cause a fall in the relative price of the nontraded good. Krueger (1974) has shown that this change in relative prices implies a drop in real income at full employment, and, therefore, a decline in real consumption.

It should be noted that, thus far, the introduction of nontraded goods has served only to make the model more complete and the workings of the adjustment mechanism clearer. It has not changed Hahn's basic result: the balance of trade improves with a devaluation if all goods and money are gross substitutes.

V MONETARY ANALYSES

As stated above, a general consensus in the literature is that the principal contribution of the elasticities-absorption debate was not that it generated a satisfactory synthesis of the two approaches (which it did not), but, rather, that it led to a rediscovery of the important role played by monetary factors in the balance of payments adjustment process. As a result of this rediscovery, and, more directly, as a result of the early work of Hahn (1959), Johnson (1958), Michaely (1960), Mundell (several papers in the early 1960s, reprinted as Parts II and III of Mundell (1968)), and Tsiang (1961), a major new approach to the analysis of payments issues has emerged. Although several distinct problems are being examined in this literature (unlike the elasticities and absorptionist literature, which focused on the short-run effects of exchange rate changes on the trade balance), and although the analytical tools differ widely, the fact that these new writings all focus on the role of asset, or wealth, changes in determining net payments positions, has led to their being grouped together under the general heading of monetary analyses of the balance of payments.

Having said this, however, it is, at least for the purposes of this study, useful immediately to identify two major subdivisions within the monetary approach—namely (1) the portfolio balance literature and (2) the monetarist literature—and to discuss the general thrust of this literature under these two subheadings.

Portfolio Balance and International Capital Movements

As the heading to this subsection indicates, the main focus of the portfolio balance literature is on the capital account of the balance of payments. While this literature had its origins in the elasticities-absorption debates, and the attempts at synthesis, it reflects more a concern over the historic limitations of the analysis to the trade account, and only as a by-product a desire to highlight the role of monetary factors in the adjustment process. In essence, this literature represents a refinement and further development of the early work of McKinnon (1969) and McKinnon and Oates (1966), and is an extension of the pioneering work by Markowitz and Tobin[25] on efficient portfolio selection to an open economy.

Like the earlier work of McKinnon and Oates, more recent studies, such as those of Allen (1973) and Branson (1970), take as their point of departure the fundamental distinction between stock and flow equilibria for various assets. In these analyses, individuals are assumed to have desired levels of holdings of the various assets available, with these levels depending, of course,

[25] The standard references here are Markowitz (1959) and Tobin (1965).

on such variables as the relative prices of all assets and the level of wealth of the individual (or nation). A steady-state stock equilibrium prevails when, for the existing vector of asset prices, desired holdings of all assets equal actual holdings, and world excess demands are zero. In such a framework, international capital flows will, obviously, be temporary phenomena, continuing only until a full portfolio stock equilibrium is reached. In a growing economy, capital flows can persist indefinitely, with such flows along steady-state growth paths reflecting the equilibrium rate of accumulation of the various assets in individual portfolios.

While the results that have thus far emerged from these analyses are both interesting and important, and while this literature represents a significant step forward in payments analysis, the portfolio balance literature will not be discussed further here. For one thing, the literature is still in its early youth, if not its infancy, and the restrictive framework employed to obtain many of the results leaves their general validity open to question. More important, however, is that this literature, focused as it is on the capital account, is not relevant to the remainder of the present study. As was noted in the introduction to this chapter, the analysis in the remaining chapters of this work is restricted to an examination of the trade account. Until the model developed below is extended to include capital account transactions, therefore, the portfolio balance literature must be classified as falling outside the present frame of reference.

The Monetarist Literature

More directly related to the analysis to be found in subsequent chapters of this study is what has become known as the monetarist literature on the payments adjustment process.[26] As with

---

[26] It has sometimes been argued that a distinction ought to be made between "monetary" and "monetarist" analyses of the balance of payments. In this case, the former term would refer to all studies that emphasize the role of

the portfolio balance literature, a number of distinct problems have been examined in the monetarist studies; however, the underlying, common thread in all of them is an explicit emphasis on the role of money and the cash-balance effect in the adjustment process. In this sense, at least, the monetarist approach is a more direct outgrowth of the elasticities-absorption debate. However, as Johnson (1972) has pointed out, in a clear departure with the absorptionist literature, recent monetarist analysis assumes (explicitly or implicitly) that the monetary changes associated with a disequilibrium in the balance of payments either are not or cannot be sterilized by the monetary authorities in the long run. This, in turn, implies that the nominal money supply in each country is an endogenous variable in the long run.

Within this broad framework, the analytical techniques have included both macroeconomic growth models, of which the works of Dornbush (1971), Frenkel (1971), Frenkel and Rodriguez (1975), Johnson (1972), and Purvis (1972) are typical, and Hahn-type Walrasian comparative static models, of which Dornbush (1973a, b) is perhaps the most representative.[27] In

money, or, more broadly, financial variables, in the adjustment process, while the latter would be restricted to those studies that accept the quantity theory formulation of the demand for money equation. While this is a distinction that may have use in some contexts, it is rejected here in favor of the division indicated above. Thus, throughout this monograph, the term "monetarist" literature is used to refer to all studies emphasizing the role of money, regardless of whether or not the Cambridge equation is used as a point of departure.

[27] It is difficult to know whether or not the early work of Mundell (1968), or of Hahn (1959) and his followers (Kemp (1970), Krueger (1974), Negishi (1968), etc.) should be included under the heading of monetarist analyses. Clearly, recent work has been inspired by, and has drawn heavily upon, these earlier contributions. In later chapters of this study, results found originally in these works have been classified as monetarist theorems. However, strictly speaking, these authors probably should be classified as precursors of the monetarist approach, in the same sense that McKinnon and Oates are the intellectual forefathers of the portfolio-balance literature. The main reason for this distinction is that in both the recent portfolio-balance and monetarist

general, as might be expected, the choice of technique has been motivated by the nature of the question being investigated. In the growth literature, the initial question concerned the impact of economic growth on the balance of payments. The traditional answer, for a small country, at least, was that growth would tend to lead to a payments deficit. The logic behind this conclusion was the Keynesian system, where imports were assumed to depend on the level of income, while exports were taken as given by the small country. The monetarist literature, by focusing attention on the liquidity demands in a growing economy, demonstrated that, under reasonable assumptions, growth leads to an overall balance of payments surplus (e.g. Frenkel 1971). Moreover, within the overall balance of payments, there is no necessary presumption as to the trends in the individual accounts. Frenkel (1971) found that, early in the growth process, the current account is in surplus while the capital account is in deficit, while the reverse occurs in later stages. (The overall balance is always in surplus.) Dornbush (1971) found that the composition of the overall account depends on the source of the increase in income (population growth or an increased capital stock) and on its disposition as between consumption and asset accumulation as well as on government financing decisions.

In the most complete of the growth papers to date, Frenkel and Rodriguez (1975) have specified what is by far the most complex model yet employed, containing as it does separate consumption, investment, and production functions, as well as interrelated asset demand functions. This model is then employed to examine the exact accounts in which both short-run and long-run adjustments in the balance of payments take

---

literatures, the emphasis has been on the long-run aspects of the adjustment process, whereas the authors just cited all tended to concentrate on the short-run portion of the problem.

place when the economy is subjected to such external shocks as a once-for-all change in the exchange rate or in the stock of (nominal) money.

Before the principal findings of the Frenkel and Rodriguez paper are summarized, it is useful first to consider the more Walrasian versions of the monetarist literature, as represented by Dornbush (1973b). In general, the major reason for employing a Hahn-type Walrasian model is that it facilitates an examination of such questions as the direction of changes in the terms of trade accompanying a devaluation, and the role of nontraded goods in the adjustment process. As with the rest of the monetarist literature, the principal distinction between the more recent contributions and those of earlier writers lies in the emphasis on long-run adjustment. Dornbush, for example, considers two types of questions in his model (1973b); (1) the impact effects of a change in a control variable, and (2) the long-run effects of such changes. The principal difference in methodology is that he employs comparative static techniques rather than a growth model, and focuses on the balance of trade rather than the overall balance of payments.

Despite these analytic differences, however, the principal conclusions of the two types of models are essentially identical. In both the growth and Walrasian versions of the monetarist literature, it is found that (1) in the long run, devaluations have no lasting impact of the balance of payments, (2) as reported by Kemp (1970), Krueger (1974), and others, in the short run, equiproportional devaluations and decreases in the nominal money supply have equal impacts on the balance of payments, and (3) in the short run, a devaluation leads to an improvement in the overall balance of payments and in the balance of trade. In the more complete model of Frenkel and Rodriguez, a devaluation also is shown (4) to lead to a short-run surplus in the capital account and a deterioration in the debt service account. Insofar as nontraded goods are concerned, Dornbush (1973b) has reconfirmed (5) the earlier results of Kemp and Krueger that the relative price of the home good declines in the devaluing country in the short run, thus leading to a shift in production away from home goods and over to traded goods.

VI CONCLUDING REMARKS

This chapter has surveyed briefly the three principal approaches to devaluation analysis found in the literature. As was noted in the introduction, in general these approaches have not yet been successfully integrated or synthesized; rather, one has displaced the other in historical progression as different aspects of the adjustment process have come to be stressed at the expense of others. In the remaining chapters of this study, this deficiency in the literature is at least partially overcome, as the elasticities and absorption approaches are fully integrated. In addition, although the lack of a sector incorporating international capital flows prevents a full integration of the monetarist literature as well, it is shown that many of the principal monetarist theorems emerge as special cases of the model developed here.

CHAPTER 2

Macroeconomic Models of Open Economies: Some Specification Problems

In Chapter 1 the macroeconomic-type general equilibrium models used in existing analyses of open economies were challenged as unsatisfactory because they are either incomplete, misspecified, or both. They are incomplete because they lack either a production sector, a monetary sector, or both, and/or because they make extremely limiting assumptions, such as fixed prices everywhere. Misspecification comes from a failure to recognize that the complete closed-economy macroeconomic model is, in effect, a one-good world. Since trade models by definition include more than one good, extending the macroeconomic framework to encompass an open economy requires more care in the definition of real variables than is usually taken.

This chapter first presents an outline of one variant of the standard, short-run, closed-economy model, which allows for price as well as output changes, then discusses the rather significant difficulties involved in extending such models to analyze open economies—difficulties that have been overlooked in most contributions in the literature.

I An Aggregate Model of the Closed Economy

Traditionally, the "complete" macro model is developed following the Hicksian interpretation and is presented in the familiar IS-LM framework. In order to focus more clearly on price as well as income changes, a Marschak-type aggregate supply–aggregate demand analysis is used here instead. This version of the model has the advantage of making price changes an explicit part of the analysis. Its major limitation is that it hides changes in the interest rate in movements along the aggregate demand curve, which is undoubtedly one reason the Hicks version is more popular in the standard texts. The two approaches are complementary, however, and for the types of questions asked here the Marschak model seems more illuminating.[1]

Aggregate Demand

The demand side of the model is given by the equations describing aggregate consumption and investment behavior and the money market relationships. In the goods markets, aggregate real consumption (C) is assumed to depend on aggregate real income (Y) and the rate of interest (i), while real investment expenditures (I) are a function of the rate of interest. It is also frequently assumed that their absolute magnitude varies with the level of income.[2] Using subscripts to denote partial derivatives, the consumption function can be written as

$$(2.1) \qquad C = C(Y, i); \quad 0 < C_Y < 1, C_i < 0,$$

and the investment function as

$$(2.2) \qquad I = I(Y, i); \quad I_Y > 0, I_i < 0.$$

In the absence of a government sector, real saving (S) is definitionally equal to income less consumption. Using equa-

---

[1] For a more complete discussion of this version of the model, see, for example, Brownlee (1950) or Marschak (1951). For a textbook treatment of this version of the model, see Branson (1972).

[2] Putting the interest rate into the consumption function and the level of income into the investment function, while not essential to the development of the analysis, is usually done in the "complete" versions of the model. It also provides a handy symmetry in the treatment of consumption and investment.

tion (2.1), this implies

$$(2.3) \qquad S \equiv Y - C(Y, i) = S(Y, i); \quad 0 < S_Y < 1, S_i > 0.$$

The equilibrium condition for the demand for goods is that savings equal investment. If a shift parameter (γ) also is included in the investment function to allow for exogenous changes in demand (this can be thought of as an increase in autonomous government spending with no taxes, if desired), then the equilibrium condition is

$$(2.4) \qquad I(Y, i) + \gamma - S(Y, i) = 0.$$

On the financial side of the economy, it is assumed that there are only two assets—money and bonds. Nominal money is issued by some government authority and is the numeraire good in the economy as well as a store of value. The demand for money is assumed to depend on the level of real income and the interest rate on bonds. This results in the familiar liquidity preference function

$$(2.5) \qquad M = \frac{m}{p} = L(Y, i); \quad 0 < L_Y < 1, L_i < 0,$$

where M is the supply of real cash balances, m the supply of nominal money, and p is the domestic price level. Equation (2.5) requires that the supply of real cash balances (M) equals the demand (L).[3]

On the assumption that m is exogenously given by the monetary authorities, equations (2.4) and (2.5) form a system of two equations in the three unknowns, Y, i, and p, and

[3] Equation (2.5) is valid only if prices do not change or under the naive assumption that, whatever the past history of price level movements, everyone believes that the existing price level will persist indefinitely. Rather than further complicate the model at this point, the latter assumption is customarily adopted. This implies a rather simple minded hypothesis about expectations, but the added complexity a more realistic assumption would entail is not worth the return at this point.

define the aggregate demand side of the economy. As long as they are independent and consistent, they can be reduced to one equation in two unknowns. Eliminating i yields,

$$(2.6) \qquad Y^d = Y^d(p),$$

where the superscript on Y indicates a demand equation. Equation (2.6) can be interpreted as the aggregate demand for real output as a function of the price level. The sign of dY^d/dp can be determined by totally differentiating (2.4) and (2.5). This gives

$$(I_Y - S_Y) \, dY^d + (I_i - S_i) \, di = - \, d\gamma$$

$$(2.7)$$

$$L_Y \, dY^d + L_i \, di = \frac{1}{p^2} [p \, dm - m \, dp].$$

Solving for dY^d yields

$$(2.8) \qquad dY^d = \frac{1}{\Delta_A} \left[\frac{1}{p^2} (p \, dm - m \, dp)(I_i - S_i) + L_i \, d\gamma \right],$$

where $\Delta_A = [L_Y(I_i - S_i) - L_i(I_Y - S_Y)]$.

Thus,

$$(2.9) \qquad \frac{dY^d}{dp} = - \frac{1}{\Delta_A} \left(\frac{m}{p^2} \right) (I_i - S_i).$$

The customary definition of stability[4] requires that $[L_Y(I_i - S_i) - L_i(I_Y - S_Y)] < 0$ and $(I_i - S_i) < 0$, so that $dY^d/dp < 0$.

As is apparent from equation (2.9), the negative slope to the aggregate demand function results from the influence on the interest rate of a change in the real value of the money supply. A drop in the price level with the supply of nominal money constant raises the real value of the money supply. This, in turn, results in a fall in the rate of interest, which leads to an

[4] See Samuelson (1965), pp. 276–283.

increase in investment (and consumption) spending, and, hence, in aggregate demand. Note that, in the absence of a wealth term in the consumption function (i.e. no real-balance effect), price changes have an effect on aggregate demand only through the effect of interest rate changes on spending.

Aggregate Supply

The model being developed applies to the short run, during which the existing stock of productive equipment is fixed. In this case, labor, which is assumed to be homogeneous and indifferent between various uses, is the only variable input. Aggregate output thus can be given by an aggregate production function of the form

$$(2.10) \qquad Y = Y(N); \quad Y_N > 0, Y_{NN} < 0$$

where N is the level of employment.

In the labor market, employers are assumed to hire workers up to the point where the marginal product of labor (Y_N) equals the real wage rate ($W = w/p$). This gives the relationship

$$(2.11) \qquad W = Y_N.$$

In the Classical version of the model, labor supply is also assumed to be a function of the real wage. In the Keynesian version of the model it is assumed that there is some contractually determined floor to the money wage rate, and that up to a point the supply of labor is infinitely elastic at this money wage rate. Beyond some level of employment, the Classical labor supply function takes over. If N^* is the level of employment, then

$$(2.12) \qquad \begin{cases} w = \bar{w} \text{ for } N \leqq N^* \\[2mm] N^s = N^s\left(\dfrac{w}{p}\right); \quad N^s_{w/p} > 0 \text{ for } N > N^*. \end{cases}$$

39

Up to full employment, equations (2.11) and (2.12) combine to give

$$(2.13) \qquad Y_N = \frac{\overline{w}}{p}.$$

Equations (2.10) and (2.13) form a two-equation system in the three unknowns Y, N, and p, and determine the aggregate supply side of the economy. By eliminating N the aggregate supply function,

$$(2.14) \qquad Y^s = Y^s(p),$$

is obtained.[5] This can be interpreted as the supply of real output as a function of the domestic price level. The slope of equation (2.14) is obtained by totally differentiating equations (2.10) and (2.13). This gives

$$Y_N \, dN = dY^s$$

$$(2.15)$$

$$Y_{NN} \, dN = \frac{1}{p^2} [p \, dw - w \, dp].$$

Solving for dY^s yields

$$(2.16) \qquad dY^s = \left[\frac{p \, dw - w \, dp}{p^2} \right] \left[\frac{Y_N}{Y_{NN}} \right]$$

so that

$$(2.17) \qquad \frac{dY^s}{dp} = - \frac{w}{p^2} \frac{Y_N}{Y_{NN}} > 0$$

and

$$(2.18) \qquad \frac{d^2 Y^s}{dp^2} = 2 \frac{w}{p^3} \frac{Y_N}{Y_{NN}} < 0.$$

[5] This is, of course, only one of a number of possible representations of the supply side of the model, albeit the most popular. One could also think of a non-neoclassical system, where most prices are "administered." In such an environment, equation (2.14) (or, more properly, its inverse) merely gives the (short-run) behavior of administered prices as the level of output varies.

The positive slope to the aggregate supply function results from the fact that, with fixed money wages, a rise in the price level lowers the real wage. This induces firms to hire more workers, which, from equation (2.10), increases output. Since diminishing returns to labor have been assumed (i.e. $Y_{NN} < 0$), this increase in output will be at a diminishing rate.

Equations (2.6) and (2.14) can be graphed in the (p, Y) plane as in Figure 2.1. The horizontal range of the aggregate supply curve in Figure 2.1 represents the extreme Keynesian case of fixed prices. Over this range, any shifts in the aggregate demand curve elicit changes in output but not in prices. This range occurs if $Y_{NN} = 0$, i.e. only if there is a range of constant returns to increased labor inputs.[6]

The same comparative static conclusions emerge from this version of the model as from the Hicksian approach, with the added result that, beyond the extreme Keynesian range of the aggregate supply function, the effects of shifts in policy parameters on real income changes are damped by the resulting price changes. Thus, solving equations (2.7) and (2.15) for the effect of a change in the nominal money supply and choosing units so that, initially, $p = 1$,

$$(2.19) \qquad \frac{dY}{dm} = \frac{1}{\Delta_B}(I_i - S_i)$$

where $\Delta_B = (m\beta)(I_i - S_i) + \Delta_A$, and $\beta = -(Y_{NN}/wY_N)$. Since

[6] It is perhaps of some interest to note that the "flat" portion of the aggregate supply curve in Figure 2.1 requires that both the demand curve for labor and the supply curve for labor be infinitely elastic at the same money wage rate, at least in the "conventional" representations of the Keynesian system (see, for example, Branson 1972). Alternatively, the Clower (1965), Barro and Grossman (1971), etc., approach, in which various markets are "off" their relevant supply and demand curves, could be assumed. In this case, increases in aggregate demand can elicit increases in aggregate supply with no changes in prices. Finally, as noted above, one can assume that the "supply" schedule is non-neoclassical in origin, and merely describes the movement of administered prices at various levels of capacity utilization.

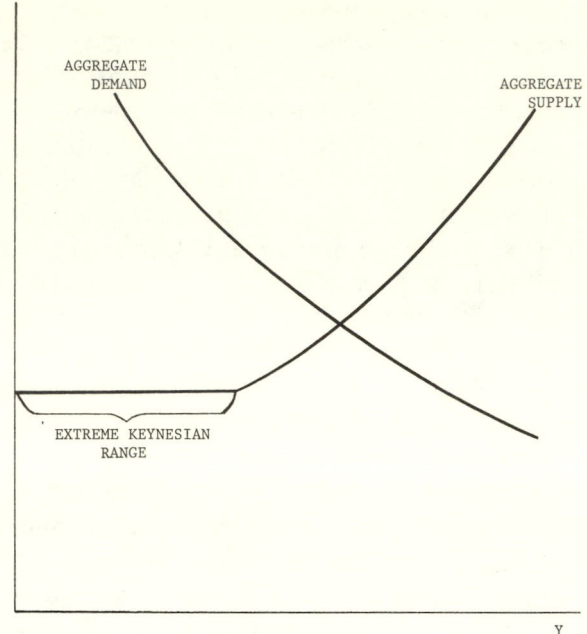

Figure 2.1

$\beta \geqq 0$, $(I_i - S_i) < 0$, and $\Delta_A < 0$, it follows that $dY/dm > 0$. In the extreme Keynesian range, $\beta = 0$, so the first term in Δ_B drops out, while outside this range, the larger is β the smaller is the response of real income to a change in the money supply.

Similarly, solving for an exogenous shift in aggregate demand results in

$$(2.20) \qquad \frac{dY}{d\gamma} = \frac{L_i}{\Delta_B} > 0,$$

and it can be seen that an increase in, say, government spending will increase the equilibrium level of real income, subject to the same dampening effects of a price change as equation (2.19).

42

In the (in)famous liquidity trap, monetary policy is ineffective while fiscal policy is still operative. This can be seen by taking the limit of equations (2.19) and (2.20) as $L_i \to \infty$ (a condition of the liquidity trap). This gives

$$(2.21) \qquad \lim_{L_i \to \infty} \frac{dY}{dm} = \lim_{L_i \to \infty} \frac{1}{\Delta_B}(I_i - S_i) = 0$$

and

$$(2.22) \qquad \lim_{L_i \to \infty} \frac{dY}{d\gamma} = \lim_{L_i \to \infty} \frac{L_i}{\Delta_B} = -\frac{1}{I_Y - S_Y} > 0.$$

Note that, in terms of Figure 2.1, both monetary and fiscal policies act to shift the aggregate demand curve to the right, but have no effect on the aggregate supply curve. In the case of a liquidity trap, the aggregate demand curve becomes vertical (under the convention that graphs price on the y axis and income on the x axis), monetary policy does not shift aggregate demand, but fiscal policy still does.[7]

II SPECIFICATION PROBLEMS OF THE OPEN-ECONOMY MODEL

Less complete variations on, and in some cases exactly, the model just developed frequently have been extended to allow for international trade. In fact, these models are the basis for the absorption literature and many of the attempted reconciliations. Unfortunately, in most instances these open-economy versions have been incorrectly specified, a problem that, if it does not invalidate, at least throws into question the applicability of many of the results obtained. It is this incorrect specification, moreover, that has been responsible

[7] The reader may verify these statements by solving equation (2.8) for dY^d/dm, $dY^d/d\gamma$, and dY^d/dp, then taking the limits of the resulting expressions as $L_i \to \infty$.

for many of the difficulties encountered by those who have attempted to integrate the various approaches to devaluation analysis.

These specification problems stem from two interrelated factors. The first is that, to make any sense at all, trade models must have at least two goods in them. The other is that the various behavioral relationships of the standard macro models are all defined in real terms. When more than one good is introduced into the model, however, considerable care must be taken to define each of the "real" variables appearing in the equations. Failure to define these real variables properly results in a misspecified model.

An examination of the modifications usually made when the model is opened to international trade will illustrate this problem. Traditionally, open-economy macro models write the equilibrium condition for the goods market as

$$(2.23) \qquad Y = C + I + (X - F),$$

where X and F are (real) exports and imports, and Y, C, and I are as previously defined. The absorptionist approach to devaluation analysis takes equation (2.23) as its point of departure. Call total domestic spending in real terms absorption (i.e. $A = C + I$), and let the net balance of trade be $B = X - F$. Then equation (2.23) can be written as

$$(2.24) \qquad Y = A + B,$$

or, rearranging

$$(2.25) \qquad B = Y - A,$$

which gives the net balance of trade as the difference between real income and absorption.

One problem that immediately arises is that the income term, Y, of equations (2.24) and (2.25) is also used as the income variable of the consumption (and investment) function. Note, however, that equation (2.24) is an equilibrium condition that requires that domestically produced output supplied (Y) equals total demand for domestically produced goods ($A + B$). Imported goods are, in fact, netted out of (2.24)–(2.25), so the measure of real income that is being used in the consumption function is simply the level of domestic (physical) production.

This point, an understanding of which is basic both to the proper specification of a macroeconomic trade model and to the analysis in Chapter 3, can perhaps be made clearer by reference to the production function. Equation (2.10), which still applies to the open-economy version of the model, defines Y as a physical quantity—the amount of aggregate output being produced by the economy. As an equilibrium condition, equation (2.24) requires that the quantity demanded of aggregate output equals the quantity supplied. This implies that imported goods are netted out of aggregate demand in equation (2.24). Thus, consumers' real income is being defined as the amount of domestically produced goods that they can purchase with their money income. When stated in this manner, it is clear that, in a two-good framework, this is not a very reasonable definition of real income.

Another way to see what is wrong with using the Y of equation (2.24) in the consumption function is to recognize that real income is actually money income divided by some price index. Money income, in turn, is simply the total quantity of each good produced multiplied by its price, with the resultant products summed over all goods. In a one-good world, if physical output is designated Q and the price of the domestic good p, then money income is pQ. Now, it seems reasonable to say that if both a domestically produced good and a foreign good are consumed, and if both p and Q remain constant, then a fall in the price of the foreign good is equivalent to a rise in real income. If, however, the Y of equation

(2.24) is used as the measure of real income, a fall in the price of the foreign good has no effect on the real income of consumers. This is because Y and Q in this case are the same.

The use of domestic physical output as the measure of the real income of consumers implies that, instead of a general price index, the price of the domestic good alone is being used to deflate money income to get a measure of real income. Likewise, since the same deflator is used throughout the model (hopefully), only the price of the domestic good is being used to deflate the nominal money supply to arrive at the real money supply. Again, in a multigood world this clearly is not a reasonable procedure. Just as real income ought to rise if the price of the foreign good (q) falls with domestic prices and output constant, so should the real value of the money supply.

To extend the model of section I, then, to the case of an open economy, it will not, in general, be sufficient simply to "tack on" an expression for the net balance of trade as is done in equation (2.23). Instead, a careful respecification of most of the equations of the model will be required to permit the incorporation of these essential distinctions. As it turns out, such a respecification automatically generates the long sought after reconciliation of the elasticities and absorption approaches as well as yielding interesting new results. It also results in an automatic inclusion of terms-of-trade effects into a macroeconomic devaluation analysis, and generates many "monetarist" results as special cases. The next chapter presents a modified model incorporating the required respecifications.

CHAPTER 3

An Integrated Macroeconomic
Model of an Open Economy

As WAS just demonstrated in Chapter 2, extending the "standard" macro model to allow for international trade is far from the trivial exercise often assumed. Moreover, with few exceptions, such an extension has not been undertaken correctly in the literature. The first part of this chapter, therefore, will develop a complete macroeconomic model of an open economy that is free of the specification errors discussed above.[1] Once the model has been developed, it will then be employed to analyze the short-run effects of a devaluation on both a fully employed and an underemployed economy. As will be seen, the model permits a derivation of these effects in more general terms than have been found hitherto in the literature. It also results in a complete integration of the elasticities and absorption approaches to devaluation analysis. Finally, a stability analysis of the model based on the Correspondence Principle is presented, and it is shown that the assumption of stability does not rule out some of the unusual results obtained.

In Chapter 4, the model will be extended so as to relax the assumption of perfect sterilization that is used in this chapter, which permits an integration of much of the monetarist literature into the model. In addition, the effects of monetary and fiscal policy will be explored. Finally, in Chapter 5, the

---

[1] In light of the complexity of the model, and in order to facilitate an heuristic explanation of its structure and working, only the small-country case is developed in the text. A formal statement of the more general two-country case can be found in Appendix A.

similarities between the single-good, aggregate model and the Hahn-type general-equilibrium models are explored; an extended Hahn model is then used to examine the further question (not tractable in a single-good framework) of the role of nontraded goods in the adjustment process.

I THE MODEL

In light of the complexities of the model developed below, it is worthwhile to outline briefly the nature of the modifications that will be introduced. Recall, first, that the standard Keynesian closed-economy model is, in effect, a one-good world. (Although the heuristic explanation of the model is in terms of NNP, prices either do not change at all or change in equal proportions, so that the Hicks composite-good theorem can be employed to treat the model as consisting of only one good.) For there to be international trade in any meaningful sense, however, there ought to be at least two goods in the system: a domestically produced good and a foreign produced good. As indicated in Chapter 2, it is the incorporation of this fact, while retaining as much of the structure of a macro model as possible, that presents most of the difficulties in extending such a model to a trading world.

In the model developed here, the domestic supply side of the system is carried over intact. Thus, the domestic and foreign economies each produce a single, all-purpose good that can be employed as a consumption good or as an investment good. The domestic and foreign goods are assumed to be (imperfect) substitutes in consumption and production, so that total demand for the domestically produced good will be the sum of home demand and foreign (i.e. export) demand. Total domestic demand, on the other hand, will consist of home country demand for the domestically produced good and for the foreign good (i.e. imports). When measured in money terms, total domestic demand will equal total demand for the domestically produced good only if trade is balanced. As it turns out, the key to a reconciliation of the elasticities and absorption approaches to devaluation analysis is to specify all of these demands (and supplies) in such a way as to maintain clearly the distinctions between real and money income, and real output and real income.

The structure of the model is developed in four stages. First, the extensively modified demand side is presented and explained, and the open-economy version of Chapter 2's aggregate demand curve is derived. Next, the aggregate supply side of the model is restated, and the slight open-economy modification required in the Classical case is explained. Third, a relationship unique to an open-economy model, the "balance of payments equilibrium line," is derived and explained. Finally, in a slight digression, the formal equivalence between the approach developed in the first three subsections and an approach based on an aggregate expenditure function is demonstrated.

As in Chapter 2, subscripts are used throughout this chapter (and the next) to denote partial derivatives of functions; where necessary, the superscripts d and s are used to denote demand or supply functions. The notation used throughout the chapter is as follows:

Y = domestic output in physical units,
A = money value of domestic absorption in domestic currency,
D = quantity of the domestic good demanded by domestic residents,
X = quantity of the domestic good demanded by foreign residents (exports),
F = quantity of the foreign good demanded by domestic residents (imports),

$\bar{Y}$ = real income,
M = supply of real cash balances,
L = demand for real cash balances,
N = labor,
p = domestic currency price of the domestic good,
q = foreign currency price of the foreign good,
e = exchange rate,
y = money income,
m = nominal money supply,
i = interest rate,
w = money wage rate,
α = $\dfrac{pD}{A}$ = share of domestic goods in total absorption,
Φ = price index.

Any additional notation will be defined as it is introduced.

Aggregate Demand

As in the closed economy, the aggregate demand side of the model consists of equations defining consumption, investment, and money demands. In addition, since the model is of an open economy, there are equations for export demand and import demand. In order to simplify the notation, consumption and investment have been lumped together as domestic absorption. This, in turn, implies that both the domestic good and the foreign good can be used for consumption and investment. The demand side of the economy then consists of the following ten equations:

$$(3.1) \qquad Y = \frac{A}{p} + \frac{B}{p},$$

$$(3.2) \qquad A = pD + eqF,$$

$$(3.3) \qquad B = pX - eqF,$$

$$(3.4) \qquad D = D(y, p, eq, i); 0 < D_y < 1,$$
$$D_p < 0, D_{eq} = ?, D_i < 0,$$

$$(3.5) \qquad F = F(y, p, eq, i); 0 < F_y < 1,$$
$$F_p = ?, F_{eq} < 0, F_i < 0,$$

$$(3.6) \qquad X = X(p/e); X_{p/e} < 0,$$

$$(3.7) \qquad M = m/\Phi = L(\bar{Y}, i); 0 < L_Y < 1, L_i < 0,$$

$$(3.8) \qquad y = pY,$$

$$(3.9) \qquad \bar{Y} = y/\Phi,$$

$$(3.10) \qquad \Phi = \alpha p + (1 - \alpha)eq.$$

As an equation on the demand side of the model, (3.1) is an accounting identity defining the quantity demanded of the domestic good as the value of domestic absorption plus the balance of trade in domestic currency, both divided by the price of the domestic good.[2] Equations (3.2) and (3.3) also are accounting identities. Equation (3.2) gives the money (nominal) value of absorption as the sum of domestic spending on the domestic good plus domestic spending on the foreign good. Equation (3.3) gives the net balance of trade in money terms as the value of exports less the value of imports.[3] Home country demand for the domestic good and the foreign good is given by equations (3.4) and (3.5). These equations are cast as standard microeconomic demand functions, and, where necessary, it will be assumed that the standard microeconomic

[2] Equation (3.1) will become an equilibrium condition when the aggregate supply side of the model is specified, and it is required that quantity demanded equal quantity supplied. At this point, however, it is not yet anything more than a demand identity.

[3] Substitution of equations (3.2) and (3.3) into (3.1) will make clear the fact that the latter is in fact a measure of the quantity of the domestic good demanded. The value of imports in fact cancels out of equation (3.1).

51

properties apply to them.[4] Specifically, it is assumed that they are homogeneous of degree zero in money income and prices,[5] and that the effects of a price change on quantity demanded can be broken down into an income and a substitution effect. Equation (3.6) gives demand for exports as a function of their price in units of the foreign currency.[6]

The money market is represented by the standard Keynesian liquidity preference function, with equation (3.7) requiring that the demand for real cash balances, as given by the liquidity preference function, L, equal the supply.[7] The absence of any demand for foreign real cash balances by domestic residents reflects the fact that the model examines only goods trade, and assumes no capital flows. The last three equations are definitions of money income (price multiplied by quantity of the domestic good, equation (3.8)); real income (money income divided by a price index, equation (3.9)); and the price index (a weighted average of the prices of the domestic good and the foreign good, the weights being the share of each in total

---

[4] This, of course, implies an assumption that aggregate functions behave like micro ones, which is not true in general. However, Pearce (1962) argues that the conditions necessary for this assumption to be a reasonable one are, in fact, not as stringent as is commonly thought. However, in what follows, whenever the Slutsky decomposition effect is used to obtain a result, an equivalent result can be obtained by making an assumption about the relative strength of gross price effects.

[5] Since the homogeneity assumption implies that any price can be used as a numeraire in the system, the thoughtful reader may wonder what has happened to the objections raised in Chapter 2. The answer is that, in this version of the model the demand for money requires a price index to be adequately specified. Below, where the model is recast in terms of an aggregate expenditure function, equation (3.10) is necessary to specify both real expenditures and the demand for real cash balances.

[6] Throughout this chapter and the next it is assumed that foreign prices, incomes and interest rates remain constant. This can be justified by assuming that any tendency for them to change is immediately offset by foreign fiscal and monetary policy.

[7] The native expectations assumption again is used to justify equation (3.7).

52

absorption, equation (3.10)). In working through the analysis, units have been chosen initially so as to normalize all prices and the exchange rate at unity.

As has been pointed out, the principal changes required on the demand side of the model center on distinctions between physical, "real," and monetary variables. In definitional terms this is done in equations (3.8) through (3.10), with the price deflator explicitly taking account of the fact that the imported good is consumed. In behavioral terms, there are two possible ways of specifying functions for the demand for goods. One is to specify explicitly separate demand equations for each good in the system. The other is to specify an aggregate expenditure function and a specific import demand function. Although the latter approach is the traditional one, the former has been adopted here. However, at the end of this section the relationship between the two approaches will be developed. In section II this relationship will be employed to present the results of the devaluation analysis in terms of the two formulations and any differences between them will be discussed in some detail.

Since e and m are exogenous,[8] and q is assumed fixed, by taking p as a parameter, equations (3.1) through (3.4) and (3.6) through (3.10) can be reduced to a single equation in Y and p.[9] This gives

$$(3.11) \qquad Y^d = Y^d(p).$$

Analogous to equation (2.6) for the closed-economy model, equation (3.11) can be interpreted as giving aggregate demand

[8] The assumption that m is exogenous in an open-economy model implies the assumption that the monetary authorities are following a policy of complete sterilization of international transactions. That is, changes in official reserves resulting from a deficit or surplus are offset so as to keep the nominal money supply constant within the country. This assumption will be relaxed in Chapter 4.

[9] Equation (3.5) is not needed since imports net out of the system. See footnote 3.

for the domestic good as a function of its price. The slope of (3.11) is found by totally differentiating the underlying equations and solving for dY^d/dp to obtain[10]

$$(3.12) \qquad \frac{dY^d}{dp} = \frac{1}{\Delta_1}\left[X_{p/e} - D_{eq} - \frac{D_i}{L_i}(\alpha m + (1 - \alpha)yL_{\bar{Y}})\right],$$

where $\Delta_1 = 1 - D_y + (D_i/L_i)L_Y > 0$.

Equation (3.12) is the open-economy counterpart to equation (2.9) of Chapter 2. In the closed economy, it will be recalled, the negative slope to the aggregate demand function resulted from the fact that an increase in the price level reduced the real value of the money supply, which in turn led to an increase in the interest rate and a drop in the interest-sensitive component of aggregate expenditure. In an open economy, this indirect interest rate effect is still present (i.e. in $-(D_i/L_i)(\alpha m + (1 - \alpha)yL_{\bar{Y}})$); however, in addition there is a direct effect as the increase in the price of the domestic good reduces exports and induces domestic residents to shift their expenditure away from the domestically produced good and over to imports. Note, however, that, to guarantee the sign of dY^d/dp, an additional assumption must be made, which is the first significant difference between the open- and the closed-economy models. Specifically, to insure that the aggregate demand curve has a negative slope, it must be assumed that the domestic and foreign goods are gross substitutes. Since the signs of all other terms are known, if the domestic and foreign goods are gross substitutes (i.e. $D_{eq} > 0$), then $dY^d/dp < 0$. If they are not gross substitutes, then $dY^d/dp < 0$ if

$$(3.12a) \qquad \left|X_{p/e} - \delta_{eq} - \frac{D_i}{L_i}(\alpha m + (1 - \alpha)yL_{\bar{Y}})\right| > |FD_y|,$$

[10] The derivations of all equations presented in the text can be found in Appendix A.

where δ_{eq} is the cross-price substitution effect in the Slutsky decomposition. Condition (3.12a) asserts that, if the domestic and foreign goods are not gross substitutes, then the slope of the aggregate demand curve for the domestically produced good will be negative if the sum of the direct effect of the price change on exports plus the income-compensated effect of the price change on the domestic demand for the domestically produced good plus the indirect interest rate effect exceeds, in absolute value, the income effect of the price change on the domestic demand for the domestically produced good. In the rest of this chapter it will be assumed that $dY^d/dp < 0$, which is clearly the most likely case. Note, however, that $dY^d/dp > 0$ is by no means impossible from an economic standpoint. If, say, domestic demand is insensitive to the interest rate, so that $D_i = 0$, while exports are relatively insensitive to price changes, so that $X_{p/e}$ is "small," then if gross substitutability does not hold, it is possible for $|X_{p/e} - \delta_{eq}| < |FD_y|$. This might be the case in a small country producing and exporting mostly agricultural raw materials.

Aggregate Supply

If all of the assumptions of Chapter 2 are retained, aggregate supply of the domestically produced good is determined by the three equations

(3.13) $Y = Y(N); \quad Y_N > 0, Y_{NN} < 0,$

(3.14) $Y_N = \left(\dfrac{w}{p}\right),$

and

(3.15) $\begin{cases} w = \bar{w} \ (\text{Keynesian case}) \\[2mm] N^s = N^s\left(\dfrac{w}{\Phi}\right); \quad N^s_{w/} > 0 \ (\text{Classical case}), \end{cases}$

where equation (3.13) is the production function, (3.14) the requirement that the money wage rate equal the value of the marginal product of labor, and (3.15) the labor supply function. In the Keynesian case, the labor "supply" function remains unchanged from the closed-economy model. In the Classical system, however, since labor supply is assumed to be responsive to the real wage, it is necessary to divide the money rate by the price index Φ (given by equation (3.10)), rather than by the price of the domestic good, p, in order to obtain the correct labor supply function. As in Chapter 2, labor supply is still a positive function of the real wage.

Since the Keynesian case is the same system as in Chapter 2, by assuming that $w = \bar{w}$, equations (3.13) through (3.15) can be reduced to[11]

$$(3.16) \qquad Y^s = Y^s(p); \quad Y^s_p > 0, Y^s_{pp} < 0.$$

The supply side of the model is included for the sake of logical completeness. As will be shown later, in a Keynesian less-than-full employment model, its inclusion does not seriously affect the results of the analysis. In fact, a more general theory of price determination not relying on marginal productivity theory could be used in this case merely by specifying a function of the form

$$(3.16a) \qquad p = p(Y); \quad p_Y \geqq 0.$$

This could then be interpreted as saying that prices rise as producers move toward some crucial rate of capacity utilization of plant, for example. In section III, however, where an examination of the properties of the model under Classical conditions is presented, the explicit inclusion of a supply sector complete with labor market and production function turns out to be essential to the analysis.

[11] The Classical supply function will be developed in section III.

Balance of Payments Equilibrium Line

In the open-economy model a third relationship, in addition to the aggregate supply and demand functions, can be defined. This is the locus of (p, Y) combinations for which trade is balanced (i.e. for which $B = 0$). This locus can be found by setting the right-hand side of equation (3.3) equal to zero, then reducing it and equations (3.5) through (3.10) to a single implicit equation in Y, p, e, and m. Since e and m are given exogenously, if the conditions of the implicit function theorem are met this can be solved to give

$$(3.17) \qquad Y^B = Y^B(p),$$

where Y^B indicates the level of output for which trade is balanced, given p. Solving for the slope of equation (3.17) as in the aggregate supply and demand equations yields

$$(3.18) \qquad \frac{dY^B}{dp} = \frac{1}{\Delta_2}\left[X(1 + \eta_X + \eta_F) \right.$$

$$\left. + \frac{F_i}{L_i}(\alpha m + (1 - \alpha)yL_{\bar{Y}}) \right]$$

where $\Delta_2 = F_y - (F_i/L_i)L_{\bar{Y}}$, and η_X and η_F are the own-price elasticities of demand for exports and imports, defined negatively. The term $(1 + \eta_X + \eta_F)$ is, of course, the Marshall-Lerner expression.

A quick examination of equation (3.18) reveals that the sign of dY^B/dp is ambiguous, with the sign of both the numerator and denominator indeterminate a priori. Fortunately, the several possible cases can be given straightforward economic interpretations and do not seem to involve any unreasonable or perverse behavior. Since equation (3.18) involves several interactions, an interpretation is presented in stages.

Assume first that import demand is unresponsive to changes in the interest rate, so that $F_i = 0$. If this is true, then equation

(3.18) reduces to

$$\text{(3.18a)} \qquad \frac{dY^B}{dp} = \frac{1}{F_y} [X(1 + \eta_X + \eta_F)],$$

and only two cases are possible: (a) the Marshall-Lerner condition is met or (b) it is not. Under condition (a), $dY^B/dp < 0$ whereas under (b) $dY^B/dp > 0$. In this case ($F_i = 0$), equation (3.18a) can be given a simple diagramatic interpretation. In Figures 3.1 and 3.2 the loci of (p, Y) combinations for which $B = 0$ are drawn with a negative and a positive slope, respectively. In both cases assume the balance of trade is in equilibrium at point A or A'. In Figure 3.1 the Marshall-Lerner

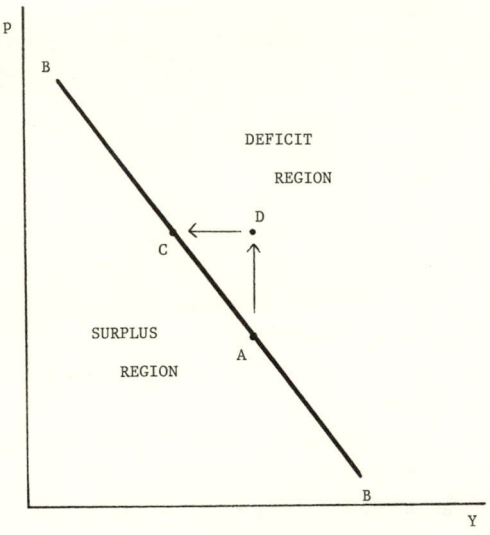

Figure 3.1

condition is met. In this case, an increase in p causes the economy to move into a deficit region, to, say, point D. This results from two factors: (i) the increase in p with Y constant causes money income to rise, thus increasing imports—this is

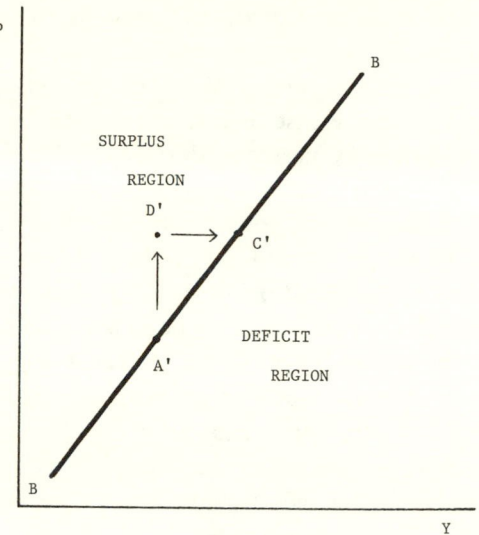

Figure 3.2

captured in the F_y term of the denominator, and may be referred to as the nominal income effect of the price change; (ii) the increase in p causes a shift in spending away from domestic goods and over to foreign goods, which, since the Marshall-Lerner condition is met, implies a deterioration in the trade balance. To restore balanced trade in this case requires that output fall, which will lower income and imports, and thus move the economy to point C.

In Figure 3.2, the Marshall-Lerner condition is not met. In this case the increase in p which moves the economy to D' implies that a surplus has developed. Note that the income effect of the price change still pulls for a deficit, but it is outweighed by the fact that, with the Marshall-Lerner condition not holding, the value of exports relative to imports is going up. In this case, to restore equilibrium requires an increase in Y, and thus in income and imports, so as to eliminate the surplus.

Another way to look at this is to note that an increase in output and income, with prices constant, always moves the economy into a deficit region. Whether the deficit will be corrected by a price increase or decrease depends on whether or not the Marshall-Lerner condition is met. If it is, a price decrease is required to generate a surplus; if it is not, an increase in the price of the domestic good has to take place.

Relaxing the assumption that $F_i = 0$ (or $L_i \to \infty$) rapidly complicates the interpretation of equation (3.18). To begin with, a term reflecting interest rate effects is added in both the numerator and denominator. These interest rate effects also go in with the opposite sign. Fortunately this is fairly easy to explain, since one term represents the effect of an increase in p on the interest rate assuming that the price index does not change, while the other reflects the effect on the interest rate of the change in the price index as p changes, all other variables held constant. In the denominator, note the term $-(F_i/L_i)L_{\bar{y}}$. As p increases, with Y fixed, money income rises. If Φ did not change, real income also would rise, and, with a constant money supply, so would the interest rate. This interest rate effect tends to lower imports by the assumption that $F_i < 0$. In the numerator, the term $(F_i/L_i)[\alpha m + (1 - \alpha)L_{\bar{y}}]$ takes account of the fact that the increase in p also increases Φ, thus lowering both the real value of the money supply and the demand for money (by lowering real income). On balance, the net effect of the change in p is to increase the interest rate, since money income increases by more than the price index (therefore raising real income) and the real value of the money supply falls. The combination of all these effects causes the interest rate to rise and, therefore, the level of imports to fall.

The fact that the interest rate effect moves opposite to the income effect clearly complicates the interpretation of (3.18). As an aid to understanding the various interactions, consider the (admittedly unrealistic) case of no income effect on imports, and demand elasticities that sum to unity—i.e. assume that $\eta_X + \eta_F = -1$ and $F_y = 0$. Then (3.18) becomes

$$(3.18b) \qquad \frac{dY^B}{dp} = -\frac{1}{L_{\bar{Y}}}[\alpha m + (1 - \alpha)yL_{\bar{Y}}],$$

and the slope of the balance of payments equilibrium line clearly will be negative. Figure 3.3 can be used to show what is happening. Moving from point A to point D implies that real income has risen and with it the interest rate. Since only interest rate changes affect imports, imports fall, thus generating a surplus. To restore equilibrium requires a drop in prices, hence in income and the interest rate, and an increase in imports again until the economy gets to point C. Note that,

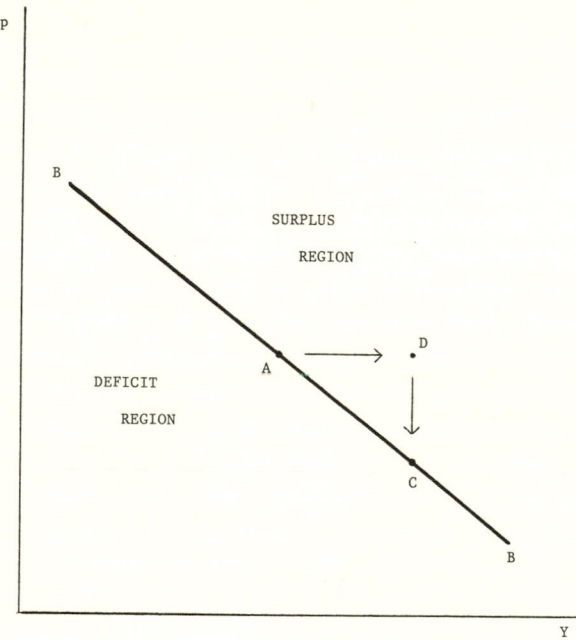

Figure 3.3

without direct income effects an increase in income leads to a surplus, whereas before it generated a deficit.

If it is assumed that $F_y > 0$, and $\eta_X + \eta_F \neq -1$, the situation becomes even more complex. Suppose, first, that $\Delta_2 < 0$, so that interest rate effects dominate income effects. If the Marshall-Lerner condition is not met, then $dY^B/dp < 0$. This case also can be explained with the aid of Figure 3.3. Suppose Y increases, moving the economy from point A to point D. With p constant, income and the interest rate rise. Since $\Delta_2 < 0$, interest rate effects dominate, and a surplus develops. To eliminate the surplus requires that p fall. This will generate a deficit via both the elasticity effects and the fact that the lower income will lead to lower interest rates, which raises imports again. This will move the economy to a new equilibrium at C.

If the Marshall-Lerner condition holds, then the slope of dY^B/dp depends on whether or not the elasticity effects dominate interest rate effects. If they do, the slope is positive, with a surplus region to the right of the locus again, and a deficit to the left. It is also possible to carry out the same analysis under the assumption that $\Delta_2 > 0$, but to do so would become boringly taxonomic.[12]

Two general points can be made about all the cases. First, whether or not an increase in output (and hence income) with prices constant will generate a surplus or a deficit depends on a complex set of interactions between income, elasticity, and interest rate effects; second, and more important, it is possible under some circumstances to have a positively sloped balance of payments equilibrium line. This in turn implies the possibility of multiple "equilibria" in the sense of more than one

---

[12] The most likely case would seem to be $\Delta_2 > 0$, with the Marshall-Lerner condition holding, and income plus elasticities effects dominating interest rate effects. Diagrammatically this is the same as the world portrayed by Figure 3.1.

(p, Y) combination consistent with balanced trade and equality of aggregate demand and supply. For example, in Figure 3.4 a policy maker presumably would prefer to be at A′ rather than A since A′ represents a higher level of domestic production, and hence employment, than does point A.

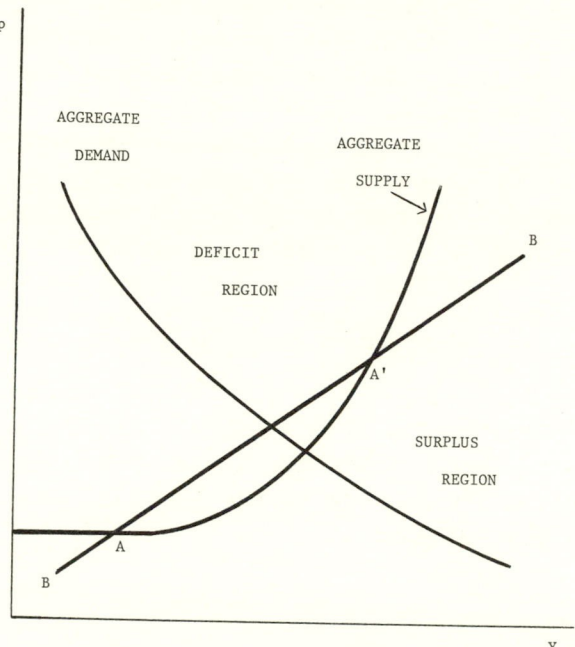

Figure 3.4

In the remainder of this study it will be assumed that the balance of payments equilibrium line is negatively sloped, so that there is a unique equilibrium. However, it should be kept in mind that this is, in fact, a special case, and that the possibility of multiple equilibria exists.

The Aggregate Expenditure Function

As was mentioned before, most studies of this sort are carried out in terms of an aggregate expenditure function and an import demand function. It is this formulation that yields the familiar modified Marshall-Lerner condition that requires that the sum of the elasticities of demand for exports and imports exceed unity plus the marginal propensity to import. The specification of separate demand equations for each good turns out not to yield exactly this condition. However, since the analysis here (and in most of the literature) begins by assuming that the economy is at a point of balanced trade, and that initially all prices are equal to unity, there is a straightforward relationship between the two specifications.

Assume that the expenditure patterns of the economy are representable by an aggregate absorption function of the form

$$(3.19) \qquad \bar{A} = \bar{A}(\bar{Y}, i); \quad 0 < \bar{A}_{\bar{Y}}(<1), \bar{A}_i < 0,$$

where $\bar{A}$ is real absorption (i.e. $\bar{A} = A/\Phi$). On the assumption that money absorption (A) is still given by equation (3.2), the implied relationship between equations (3.19) and (3.4) can be found by totally differentiating equation (3.19). This yields, after some rearrangement,

$$(3.20) \qquad dA = \bar{A}_{\bar{Y}}\, dy + \left(1 - \frac{y}{A}\, \bar{A}_{\bar{Y}} \right) A\, d\Phi + \bar{A}_i\, di.$$

Note that $dA = d(pD + eqF)$ (from equation (3.2)), and that $A\, d\Phi = A(\alpha\, dp + (1 - \alpha)\, de)$. Since $p = e = q = 1, \alpha = D/A$ and $(1 - \alpha) = F/A$, so that equation (3.20) becomes

$$(3.21) \qquad dD + dF + D\, dp + F\, de$$
$$= \bar{A}_{\bar{Y}}\, dy + \left(1 - \frac{y}{A}\, \bar{A}_{\bar{Y}} \right)(D\, dp + F\, de) + \bar{A}_i\, di,$$

or

(3.21a) $dD + dF = \bar{A}_{\bar{Y}}\, dy$

$$- y\bar{A}_{\bar{Y}}(\alpha\, dp + (1 - \alpha)\, de) + \bar{A}_i\, di.$$

From equation (3.5) it follows that $dF = F_y\, dy + F_p\, dp + F_{eq}\, de + F_i\, di$, which together with equation (3.21a), implies that

(3.22) $dD = (\bar{A}_{\bar{Y}} - F_y)\, dy - (\alpha y\bar{A}_{\bar{Y}} + F_p)\, dp$

$$- [(1 - \alpha)y\bar{A}_{\bar{Y}} + F_{eq}]\, de + (\bar{A}_i - F_i)\, di.$$

While this does not violate any of the usual microeconomic assumptions about the signs of various derivatives, (e.g. it is still true that $D_y > 0$), it certainly does impose added conditions on the nature of the demand functions. Whether these are more or less restrictive than an assumption that demand functions for an economy have the same properties as do those for an individual appears to be an open question. Nevertheless, the separate demand function specification would appear to be the more general one, since it is independent of the assumption that the Slutsky decomposition applies to the aggregate functions.[13] In what follows, equation (3.22) will be used to compare all results obtained using the demand system specified by equations (3.1) through (3.10) with those that would follow from the alternative aggregate expenditure function specification.

II   Devaluation, Employment and the Balance of Trade in a Keynesian World

In this section, the model just developed is employed to examine the short-run effects of a devaluation on both domestic

---

[13] Although the Slutsky decomposition is in fact employed to examine various possible cases in what follows, it is not necessary to the analysis. If it does not hold in the aggregate, then equivalent statements in terms of gross price effects can be made.

production and the balance of trade. In the analysis, a general expression giving the effect of a devaluation on the trade balance is derived that completely integrates the elasticities and absorption approaches. In addition, the assumptions implicit in the use of an aggregate expenditure (or absorption) function are used to convert the results obtained in the more general specification over to this framework. As has been argued elsewhere in literature (e.g. Dornbush 1973b, Vanek 1962), the analysis shows that the famous Marshall-Lerner condition is sufficient for a devaluation to improve the trade balance only in some restrictive special cases. In a general framework, however, it is neither necessary nor sufficient for there to be an improvement in the trade balance, although it does appear in the final expression. However, although neither necessary nor sufficient in the general case, other things equal if the Marshall-Lerner condition is met then the overall sufficiency condition is easier to fulfill. Another result that emerges from the model is that it is possible (if the authorities follow an orthodox neutral monetary policy) for a devaluation to lead to a drop in the level of output and employment even if the trade balance improves.

Employment Effects

The Keynesian version of the model developed above assumes that the money wage rate, w, is institutionally fixed. In this case, the supply of labor is infinitely elastic at the going money wage rate, and changes in the level of employment come about through shifts in the demand curve for labor. Demand for labor, in turn, is positively related to demand for the domestic good. Thus, if the impact of a devaluation on the equilibrium level of output can be determined (i.e. if the sign of dY/de can be determined), its impact on employment is also known.

The effect of a devaluation on the equilibrium quantity of the domestic good produced can be obtained by totally differentiating equations (3.1) through (3.10) and (3.13) through (3.16), reducing them to a system of three equations in the three endogenous variables Y, i, and B and the exogenous variables m and e, and then solving for dY/de by Cramer's Rule. This gives (after rearranging of terms)

$$(3.23) \qquad \frac{dY}{de} = \frac{1}{\Delta_3}\left[D_{eq} - X_{p/e} - \frac{D_i}{L_i} m(1 - \alpha)(1 - \mu)\right]$$

where $\Delta_3 = \{1 - D_y - \beta(X_{p/e} - D_{eq}) + (D_i/L_i)[L_{\bar{Y}} + \beta(\alpha m + (1 - \alpha)yL_{\bar{Y}})]\}$, $\beta = -Y_{NN}/Y_N^2$), and μ is the income elasticity of demand for real cash balances. Since $\beta \geqq 0, \Delta_3 > 0$ as long as the aggregate demand curve has a negative slope,[14] or, equivalently, as long as the (second) condition for the model to be stable (derived in section IV below) is met.

Unfortunately, while the sign of the denominator is relatively easy to pin down, the sign of the numerator is much more ambiguous. In the first place, it is necessary to determine the magnitude of a variable prominent in the work of Friedman—the income elasticity of demand for real cash balances (μ). Moreover, even if the size of μ can be established, the sign of (3.23) is still uncertain. Thus, a number of cases must be considered. However, what emerges from these various cases is the somewhat surprising result that, under not unreasonable conditions, a devaluation can reduce the level of output and employment in the devaluing country.

Assume, first, that Friedman is correct, and that μ can be taken to be precisely unity. In this case, $dY/de > 0$ if the domestic and foreign goods are gross substitutes (i.e. if $D_{eq} > 0$).

---

[14] A rearrangement of terms in Δ_3 gives: $\Delta_3 = 1 - D_y + (D_i/L_i) L_{\bar{Y}} - \beta[X_{p/e} - D_{eq} - (D_i/L_i)(\alpha m + (1 - \alpha)yL_Y)]$. The bracketed term must be negative for $dY^d/dp < 0$. As long as it is negative, $\Delta_3 > 0$.

If they are not gross substitutes, then under the assumption that the Slutsky theorem can be used to break D_{eq} down into income and substitution effects, $D_{eq} = \delta_{eq} - FD_y$. If $\mu = 1$, then

$$(3.24) \qquad \frac{dY}{de} \gtreqless 0 \quad \text{as} \quad |\delta_{eq} - X_{p/e}| \quad |FD_y|.$$

This condition can be given a straightforward interpretation in terms of the familiar Hicksian IS and LM curves, modified so as to put domestic output, rather than "real" income, along the horizontal axis. In general, if $\mu \neq 1$, a devaluation will cause both the IS and the LM curves to shift. That is, the direct effects of a devaluation will be felt in both the goods market and the money market. If $\mu \equiv 1$, however, the LM curve does not shift with a devaluation. This is because the impact effect of the devaluation is to lower both real income and the real value of the money supply (the nominal money supply held constant) by the same amount. With the income elasticity of demand for real money equal to unity, no change in the demand for money occurs, and the LM curve remains fixed. Thus, whether aggregate demand for the domestically produced good, and, hence, whether domestic real output and employment, rises or falls depends on whether the IS curve shifts to the right or to the left. This, in turn, depends on whether or not the increase in aggregate demand for the domestic good resulting from the increase in exports is reinforced by a shift in domestic demand away from the foreign good and over to the domestically produced good, or is offset by a net drop in domestic demand for the domestic good as a result of unfavorable income effects. If gross substitutability holds, then $dY/de > 0$. If, however, the domestic and foreign goods are not gross substitutes, then condition (3.24) states that domestic output and employment will decline if the (negative) income effect of the

68

devaluation is large enough to offset the combined substitution effect and the effect on exports.[15]

If $\mu \neq 1$, then both the conditions necessary to establish the sign of equation (3.23) and the interpretation of these conditions become more complex. Consider first the case where $\mu < 1$. If the domestic and foreign goods are gross substitutes, then

$$(3.25) \qquad \frac{dY}{de} \gtreqless 0 \quad \text{as} \quad |D_{eq} - X_{p/e}|$$

$$\gtreqless \left| (1 - \alpha)(1 - \mu)m \frac{D_i}{L_i} \right|.$$

Condition (3.25) asserts that whether or not a devaluation will lead to an increase or a decrease in output depends on whether or not the goods market effects dominate the money market effects. Again, this can be readily explained in terms of shifts in IS and LM curves.

If $\mu < 1$, then a devaluation shifts the LM curve to the left. This follows because the demand for real cash balances is not dropping in proportion to the decline in the real value of the money supply. With domestic and foreign goods gross substitutes, the IS curve shifts unambiguously to the right. Thus, whether domestic output rises or falls depends on whether or not the effects of the rightward shift of the IS curve more than offset the effects of the leftward shift of the LM curve. Note also that the term $(1 - \alpha)$, the share of imports in total domestic spending, influences the sign of equation (3.23). Other things equal, the larger is the share of imports in total domestic spending the greater is the tendency for output and employment to decline with a devaluation. This is because the size of $d\Phi/de$

---

[15] Note that $dY/de < 0$ does not violate the stability conditions derived below. Nor does it require "unusual" shapes for the demand curve. With $\mu \equiv 1$, the demand curve is negatively sloped if $|X_{p/e} - \delta_{eq} - (D_i/L_i)m| > |FD_y|$. Clearly, it is possible to have $dY^d/dp < 0$ and $dY/de < 0$ at the same time.

depends directly on the magnitude of $(1 - \alpha)$. With the supply of nominal money constant, the larger is $d\Phi/de$, the greater is the leftward shift in the LM curve (ie, the greater are the effects on the money market of a devaluation).[16]

Note that, if the domestic and foreign goods are not gross substitutes, and if $\mu < 1$, the possibility that a devaluation will have negative output effects is increased. In this case, the negative income effects of the devaluation on the domestic demand for domestically produced goods is added to the negative money market effects, and the condition determining the sign of equation (3.23) becomes

$$(3.26) \qquad \frac{dY}{de} \gtreqless 0 \quad \text{as} \quad \left| \delta_{eq} - X_{p/e} \right|$$

$$\left| (1 - \alpha)(1 - \mu)m \frac{D_i}{L_i} + FD_y \right|.$$

As a corollary to this, if domestic output falls, the price of the domestic good will fall as well. This can be seen by examining Figure 3.5. If the aggregate demand curve is initially either DD or $D_1 D_1$, and the devaluation lowers domestic output, this says that the demand curve is being shifted to the left. In these cases, the price of the domestic good falls as well. This fall in price has the effect, of course, of reducing the drop in output, since the leftward shift of the demand curve is partially offset by the movement to the southeast along it. In the traditional Keynesian case, where $Y_{NN} = 0$, and prices do not change (i.e. the aggregate supply function is infinitely elastic) the drop in output is even greater. This is also apparent from equation (3.23). In this range of the production function

---

[16] This follows from the assumption that the income elasticity of demand for money is less than unity. A 10 percent increase in Φ causes both the real value of the money supply and real income to drop by 10 percent. However, with $\mu < 1$, the quantity of money demanded falls by less than 10 percent, thus leading to a shift in the *LM* curve.

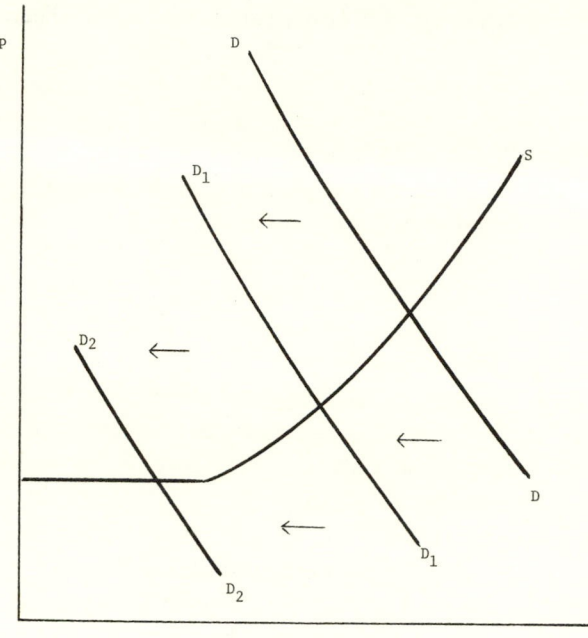

Figure 3.5

$\beta = 0$, so that $\Delta_3 = 1 - D_y + (D_i/L_i)L_{\bar{Y}}$, a smaller value than in the general case.

By making use of equation (3.22), it is possible to show that this possibility also holds for the absorption function specification of the model. From equation (3.22) observe that $D_{eq} = -(F\bar{A}_{\bar{Y}} + F_{eq})$ and $D_i = \bar{A}_i - F_i$. Substituting these into equation (3.23), and remembering that $X = F$ results in

$$(3.27) \qquad \frac{dY}{de} = -\frac{1}{\Delta_3}[X(\bar{A}_{\bar{Y}} + \eta_X + \eta_F)$$

$$+ \psi m(1 - \alpha)(1 - \mu)]$$

where $\psi = (\bar{A}_i - F_i)/L_i$. Since $\bar{A}_{\bar{Y}}$ is the marginal propensity to spend (or absorb) in real terms, $\bar{A}_{\bar{Y}} = 1 - h$, where h is the marginal propensity to hoard, also in real terms. Therefore,

$$(3.28) \qquad \frac{dY}{de} = -\frac{X}{\Delta_4}[1 + \eta_X + \eta_F - h + \psi \frac{m}{y}(1 - \mu)],$$

where $\Delta_4 = h + f - \beta X(1 + \eta_X + \eta_F - h) + \psi[L_{\bar{Y}} + \beta(\alpha m + (1 - \alpha)yL_{\bar{Y}})]$, and f is the marginal propensity to import. Since $\Delta_4 > 0,[17]$ the sufficient condition for $dY/de > 0$,

$$(3.29) \qquad \frac{dY}{de} \gtreqless 0 \quad \text{as} \quad |\eta_X + \eta_F - h| \gtreqless \left|1 + \psi\frac{m}{y}(1 - \mu)\right|$$

can be obtained.

In both the general and aggregate expenditure function versions of the model, the case where the income elasticity of demand for real-cash balances exceeds unity provides the fewest opportunities for $dY/de < 0$. If $\mu > 1$ and both goods are gross substitutes, then $dY/de > 0$ in equation (3.23). Even if $D_{eq} < 0$, $dY/de > 0$ only requires that $|\delta_{eq} - X_{p/e} - (1 - \alpha)(1 - \mu)m(D_i/L_i)| > |FD_y|$. Of course, the converse is still possible, but it would appear to be a highly unlikely event. In the more restrictive aggregate expenditure version, $\mu > 1$ means that the modified Marshall-Lerner condition is again sufficient to insure that output and employment rise with a devaluation. In all these cases, the reduced likelihood of a negative effect on output and employment follows from the fact that, with $\mu > 1$, the LM curve now shifts to the right with a devaluation, so that money market effects are expansionary in this case.

Finally, it is of some interest to note that, in two cases of historic interest in the literature, a negative value for dY/de is impossible as long as the aggregate demand curve for domesti-

---

[17] In this case Δ_4 can be rewritten as $\Delta_4 = h + f + \psi L_Y - \beta[X(1 + \eta_X + \eta_F - h) - \psi(\alpha m + (1 - \alpha)yL_{\bar{Y}})]$. As before, the bracketed term must be negative if $aY^d dp < 0$ (or, as will be shown later, to insure stability). Also, $(\bar{A}_i - F_i) < 0$ must hold if $D_i < 0$ holds. Therefore, $\Delta_4 > 0$.

cally produced goods has a negative slope. These are (a) no interest elasticity in the demand for goods (i.e. $D_i = F_i = 0$); (b) Keynesian neutral monetary policy (i.e. the monetary authorities vary the money supply so as to maintain a target interest rate so that $L_i \to \infty$).[18] In both these cases equation (3.23) reduces to

$$(3.30) \qquad \frac{dY}{de} = \frac{1}{\Delta_{3a}}(D_{eq} - X_{p/e}),$$

where $\Delta_{3a} = 1 - D_y + \beta(D_{eq} - X_{p/e})$. Assuming that the aggregate demand curve has a negative slope under these conditions requires that $D_{eq} - X_{p/e} > 0$,[19] which in turn implies that $dY/de > 0$. For the alternate specification of equation (3.23), if $\bar{A}_i = F_i = 0$ and/or $L_i \to \infty$, then

$$(3.31) \qquad \frac{dY}{de} = -\frac{1}{\Delta_{4a}}[X(1 + \eta_X + \eta_F - h)],$$

where $\Delta_{4a} = h + f - \beta X(1 + \eta_X + \eta_F - h)$. In this case, $dY^d/dp < 0$ requires that $1 + \eta_X + \eta_F - h < 0$, which insures that $dY/de > 0$.

Note, however, that an assumption of a negatively sloped demand curve if $\mu = 1$ or if $\mu < 1$ is not sufficient to guarantee that $dY/de > 0$. If $\mu = 1$, interest rate terms drop out of the numerator of equation (3.23). However, as long as there are interest rate effects, the condition for a negative slope to the aggregate demand curve is still given by equation (3.12a), regardless of the value of μ. Thus, with a sufficient interest

[18] This is also the condition of a liquidity trap.

[19] General equilibrium barter models have as a sufficient condition for stability that all goods be gross substitutes. In this context it becomes clear that gross substitutability is an overly strong sufficient condition to insure a negative slope to the aggregate demand curve. With a positively sloped aggregate supply curve, the stability condition is seen to be equivalent to assuming that in the aggregate the economy is a "well behaved market."

rate effect, the aggregate demand curve can have a negative slope, while $dY/de|_{\mu=1} < 0$. If $\mu < 1$, then the condition for $dY/de < 0$ can be rewritten as

$$(3.32) \qquad \frac{dY}{de} < 0 \quad \text{if} \quad \left| X_{p/e} - \delta_{eq} - \frac{D_i}{L_i}(\alpha m + (1 - \alpha)yL_{\bar{Y}}) \right|$$

$$< \left| FD_y + \frac{D_i}{L_i}m \right|.$$

Again, by comparing (3.32) with (3.12a) it can be seen that $dY^d/dp < 0$ and $dY/de < 0$ are not mutually exclusive.

Having said this, note that, although the assumption of an orthodox neutral monetary policy (i.e. peg the nominal money supply) is a common one in the literature, the Keynesian neutral monetary policy assumption would appear to be more reasonable. This follows from the fact that the interest rate is the policy variable that the monetary authorities try to influence. Money supply changes usually take place so as to achieve some target interest rate consistent with internal policies. The assumption of an orthodox neutral policy is, in effect, equivalent to assuming that no attempt is made by the authorities to use discretionary monetary policy to influence the economy. The preference for the orthodox neutral assumption in devaluation analysis seems to stem from Tsiang's observation that Keynesian neutral monetary policy leads to instability at full employment. However, as was noted above (p. 23), it is not clear that Tsiang's result is correct.[20] In any event, regardless of the stability question, an orthodox neutral policy does not appear to be the one usually followed by modern governments. If, in fact, Keynesian neutral policies are followed, then a devaluation will increase output and employment as long as the aggregate demand curve is negatively sloped.

---

[20] For a further discussion of the stability question, see section IV.

Balance of Payments Effects

The effect of a devaluation on the balance of trade can be obtained by again applying Cramer's Rule to the equations of the system. This yields, after considerable algebra,

$$
(3.33) \quad \frac{dB}{de} = -\frac{1}{\Delta_3} \left\{ [X(1 + \eta_X + \eta_F)] \right.
$$

$$
\times \left[(1 - D_y) + \frac{D_i}{L_i}(L_{\bar{Y}} + \beta m) \right]
$$

$$
+ (D_{eq} - X_{p/e})] \left[F_y - \frac{F_i}{L_i}(L_{\bar{Y}} + \beta m) \right]
$$

$$
\left. - [m(1 - \alpha)(1 - \mu)] \left[\frac{D_i}{L_i} F_y + \frac{F_i}{L_i}(1 - D_y) \right] \right\}.
$$

Equation (3.33) is the fundamental expression for the effect of an exchange rate change on the balance of trade. For the case of an aggregate expenditure function, by using equation (3.22) it can be shown that the basic result is

$$
(3.34) \quad \frac{dB}{de} = -\frac{1}{\Delta_4} \left\{ X \left[(1 + \eta_X + \eta_F)\left(h + \frac{\bar{A}_i}{L_i}(L_{\bar{Y}} + \beta m) \right) \right. \right.
$$

$$
\left. + h\left(f - \frac{F_i}{L_i}(L_{\bar{Y}} + \beta m) \right) \right]
$$

$$
\left. - m(1 - \alpha)(1 - \mu) \left[\frac{\bar{A}_i}{L_i} f + \frac{F_i}{L_i} h \right] \right\}.
$$

By virtue of the fact that equation (3.33) incorporates demand, supply, and monetary effects, automatically allows for a terms-of-trade effect via the definition of real magnitudes, and integrates the elasticities and absorption approaches to devaluation analysis, it is a completely general result. For those who prefer the aggregate-expenditure-function approach, equation (3.34) is the relevant general expression. As might have been expected, such an integration results in an extremely complex expression, since several factors interact to produce the final effect on the trade balance.

Sufficient conditions for $dB/de > 0$ can be obtained for both equations (3.33) and (3.34). However, since these equations are so complex, it is useful first to examine some popular special cases.

As is well-known, the original Marshall-Lerner condition was derived under the assumption that supply curves are infinitely elastic, which in the model used here was shown to be equivalent to assuming that $\beta = 0$. Furthermore, the condition assumes that there are no interest rate effects, so that $D_i = F_i = 0$, and that income changes do not take place, or are so small that they safely can be ignored, which is equivalent to assuming that terms in D_y, $\bar{A}_{\bar{Y}}$, and F_y drop out. In this case equations (3.33) and (3.34) both immediately reduce to

$$(3.35) \qquad \frac{dB}{de} = -X(1 + \eta_X + \eta_F).$$

Thus, the standard elasticities result is in fact a straightforward special case of either equation.

A more relevant special case is what the literature refers to as Keynesian neutral monetary policy. In this regime it is assumed that the monetary authorities continually change the nominal money supply so as to peg the interest rate. In terms of the model, this is equivalent to assuming that $D_i = F_i = 0$ and/or $L_i \to \infty$. Some authors also allow for a terms-of-trade effect when analyzing devaluations,[21] although it is not clear whether these analyses allow domestic prices to change, or if the terms-of-trade effect is merely the relative price change resulting from the exchange rate change. If domestic prices do not change, this is equivalent to assuming that $\beta = 0$, and

---

[21] See Tsiang (1961), for example.

equation (3.33) becomes

$$(3.35a) \qquad \frac{dB}{de} = -\left[X(1 + \eta_X + \eta_F) \right.$$
$$\left. + \left(\frac{F_y}{1 - D_y} \right)(D_{eq} - X_{p/e}) \right].$$

This says that $dB/de > 0$ requires that the sum of the elasticities be greater than unity plus a fraction of the difference between the (gross) cross-price effect of the exchange rate change on the quantity demanded of the domestic good and the (gross) own-price effect on quantity demanded of exports, where the fraction is the ratio of the marginal propensity to spend on imports to unity less the marginal propensity to spend on domestic goods, and where all marginal propensities are with respect to money income.

If it is assumed that the aggregate supply function has a positive slope, so that $\beta > 0$, then the equivalent result is

$$(3.35b) \qquad \frac{dB}{de} = -\frac{1}{\Delta_{3c}}\left[X(1 + \eta_X + \eta_F) \right.$$
$$\left. + \left(\frac{F_y}{1 - D_y} \right)(D_{eq} - X_{p/e}) \right],$$

where $\Delta_{3c} = \{[1 - D_y - \beta(X_{p/e} - D_{eq})]/(1 - D_y)\} > 0$. It is clear that the only effect of assuming $\beta > 0$ is that the magnitude of any improvement or deterioration in the trade balance is reduced.

Undertaking the same exercise for equation (3.34) generates what is frequently referred to as the modified Marshall-Lerner condition. Thus, assuming that $\bar{A}_i = F_i = 0$ (and/or $L_i \to \infty$) and $\beta = 0$, equation (3.34) can be reduced to

$$(3.36) \qquad \frac{dB}{de} = -\frac{1}{\Delta_{4b}}[X(1 + \eta_X + \eta_F + f)],$$

where $\Delta_{4b} = 1 + (f/h)$. If $\beta \neq 0$, then

$$(3.36a) \qquad \frac{dB}{de} = -\frac{1}{\Delta_{4c}} [X(1 + \eta_X + \eta_F + f)],$$

and $\Delta_{4c} = (1/h) [h + f - \beta X(1 + \eta_X + \eta_F - h)]$. In both cases it is clear that $dB/de > 0$ if $|\eta_X + \eta_F| > |1 + f|$, and that, as was true for equation (3.33), $\beta \neq 0$ only reduces the magnitude of dB/de.

The third case to be considered is orthodox neutral monetary policy, which, it will be remembered, involves pegging the nominal money supply and allowing the interest rate to adjust to any changes in the various parameters. This, of course, is one of the assumptions used to derive equations (3.33) and (3.34). It is at this point that the results obtained here differ most strikingly from those found in the literature. However, although the actual expression differs from many found in the literature, equations (3.33) and (3.34) are similar to earlier results insofar as both reveal that, while it does appear in the equation giving dB/de, neither the standard nor the modified Marshall-Lerner condition is necessary or sufficient to insure that a devaluation will improve the balance of trade.

Although it has not been possible to identify completely the reasons for the differences between the results obtained here and those found in other places in the literature, they seem to be the result of two facts: (1) in many cases the results found in earlier contributions in the literature were not based on the simultaneous solution of a complete model, but rather were obtained by grafting various additional effects onto a simpler basic equation; or (2) many otherwise complete models did not incorporate a production sector into the analysis.[22] In both cases, important interactions between various sectors of the economy were overlooked or omitted.

[22] As an example see Tsiang (1961).

As was true for the impact of a devaluation on the level of output and employment, to determine sufficient conditions for a devaluation to improve the trade balance requires consideration of several cases. Specifically, it is necessary to consider (1) whether $\mu \gtreqless 1$; (2) whether or not the domestic and foreign goods are gross substitutes; and (3) whether or not the (simple) Marshall-Lerner condition is met. Although not all cases will be examined here, it is both illustrative and interesting to consider a few possibilities.

Assume, first, that $\mu \equiv 1$, both goods are gross substitutes, and the Marshall-Lerner condition is met. Then the sufficient conditions for equations (3.33) and (3.34) to be positive are

$$(3.37) \qquad \left| X(1 + \eta_X + \eta_F)\left[1 - D_y + \frac{D_i}{L_i}(L_{\bar{Y}} + \beta m) \right] \right.$$
$$- (D_{eq} - X_{p/e})\left[\frac{F_i}{L_i}(L_{\bar{Y}} + \beta m) \right] \Bigg|$$
$$> \left| F_y(D_{eq} - X_{p/e}) \right|$$

and

$$(3.38) \qquad \left| (1 + \eta_X + \eta_F)\left[h + \frac{A_i}{L_i}(L_{\bar{Y}} + \beta m) \right] \right.$$
$$- h\frac{F_i}{L_i}(L_{\bar{Y}} + \beta m) \Bigg| > |h \cdot f|,$$

respectively.

This case is interesting in that it clearly shows one significant difference resulting from the introduction of interest rate effects: a positive slope to the aggregate supply function ($\beta > 0$) has an impact on the likelihood that $dB/de > 0$. In the case considered here, $\beta > 0$ serves to make the sufficient condition less stringent in the sense that it increases the value of the left-hand side of (3.37) or (3.38). This follows from the fact that the conditions assumed insure that $dY/de > 0$. Thus, only "favorable" interest rate effects—reducing import demand—are felt as the increase in the domestic price level reduces the real value of the money supply and raises interest rates.

If $\mu < 1$, the sufficient condition also is made less stringent in that the terms

$$\left| -[m(1 - \alpha)(1 - \mu)]\left[\frac{D_i}{L_i}F_y + \frac{F_i}{L_i}(1 - D_y)\right]\right|$$

or

$$\left| -\frac{m}{y}(1 - \mu)\left[\frac{\overline{A}_i}{L_i}f + \frac{F_i}{L_i}h\right]\right|$$

are added to the left-hand side of equations (3.37) and (3.38), respectively. In this case, the favorable interest rate effect resulting from the increase in aggregate demand for the domestic good is reinforced by the fact that the devaluation-induced drop in the real value of the money supply is not matched by an equal drop in demand for real-cash balances, further increasing the interest rate.

One reason for singling out these two cases is that they confirm Tsiang's (1961) results that the conditions for a successful devaluation are made less stringent when an orthodox neutral monetary policy is followed. As a comparison of equations (3.37) and (3.35b), or (3.38) and (3.36a), reveals, the inclusion of an interest rate effect makes the condition for a devaluation to lead to an improvement in the balance of trade less stringent. In fact, if the Marshall-Lerner condition is met, and if both goods are gross substitutes, it is only if $\mu > 1$ that an additional term is added to the right-hand side of the sufficient condition rather than only to the left. And even then, since terms also would have been added to the left-hand side, it is by no means obvious that the condition would be more stringent than in the no-interest-rate effects cases.

III   A CLASSICAL WORLD

The Model

Traditionally, analyses of the comparative statics properties of macroeconomic models have included consideration of what has become known as the "Classical" case. In the conventional version of the model, both money wage rates and prices are assumed to be perfectly flexible, and both the demand for and supply of labor are made functions of the real wage. In the absence of some exogenous factor causing a shift in either the labor supply or demand curves (usually a change in the capital stock, technical change, or attitudes toward leisure on the part of workers), employment, which is determined in the labor market, remains fixed. By working back through the production function, it can be seen that a given level of employment implies a given level of output. With employment fixed, the level of output is constant, with any price changes being accompanied by an equiproportional change in the money wage rate so that the real wage remains fixed. This, in turn, implies that the aggregate supply curve is simply a vertical line at the full employment (or no involuntary unemployment) level of output. Any shift in the aggregate demand schedule merely causes changes in prices and money wage rates, and has no effect on output or employment.

This interpretation of the Classical case has been carried over to open-economy models as well. An examination of the rationale behind the labor supply and demand functions, however, reveals that this interpretation is not correct for an open economy. The labor demand function is derived from the condition that, under competitive conditions, the value of the marginal product of labor must equal the money wage rate, i.e. from the requirement that $w = pY_N$, or $w/p = Y_N$. Since $Y_N = Y_N(N)$, a function only of N (given the existing stock of capital), a demand function for labor can be derived as the inverse of this condition, i.e.

$$(3.39) \qquad N^d = N^d \left(\frac{w}{p} \right); \qquad N^d_{w/p} < 0.$$

On the supply side, the arguments on individual behavior suggest that the supply of labor depends on the tradeoff between leisure and goods, which can be measured by the real wage. In a two-good world, however, the real wage is not w/p, but rather w/Φ. Thus, the labor supply function is properly written as

$$(3.40) \qquad N^s = N^s \left(\frac{w}{\Phi} \right); \qquad N^s_{w/\Phi} > 0.$$

This implies that the aggregate supply side of the model, when modified for the Classical case, ought to consist of equations (3.39) and (3.40) along with an aggregate production function

$$(3.41) \qquad Y = Y(N)$$

and a price index

$$(3.42) \qquad \Phi = \alpha p + (1 - \alpha)eq,$$

where all notation is as before.

Equations (3.39) through (3.42) form a system of four equations in the five variables w, p, Y, N, and Φ (when e and q are taken to be exogenous parameters). They can be reduced to an aggregate supply function of the form $Y^s = Y^s(p)$. When the system is totally differentiated, however, in order to solve for the slope of the aggregate supply function, it turns out that, instead of the Classical $dY^s/dp = 0$, the slope is positive. Specifically

$$(3.43) \qquad \frac{dY^s}{dp} = (1 - \alpha)w^2 N^d_{w/p} \left[\frac{N^s_{w/\Phi}}{N^d_{w/p} - N^s_{w/\Phi}} \right] > 0.$$

What this says, of course, is that there is no single level of output that can be labeled "full employment" output. All that exists in a Classical open-economy system is the absence of involuntary unemployment, with the actual level of employment and output changing as the aggregate demand curve shifts. Furthermore, since e and q enter into the aggregate supply function as exogenous variables, the aggregate supply curve itself will shift as they change.

Employment Effects of a Devaluation

Equations (3.39) through (3.42) can be solved to find the effect of a devaluation on the aggregate supply curve. Doing this yields

$$(3.44) \qquad \frac{dY^s}{de} = -(1 - \alpha)w^2 N^d_{w/p} \left[\frac{N^s_{w/\Phi}}{N^d_{w/p} - N^s_{w/\Phi}} \right]$$

$$= -\frac{dY^s}{dp} < 0,$$

which says that, when graphed in the (p, Y) plane, the aggregate supply curve unambiguously shifts to the left with a devaluation. This result is readily explainable via a more careful consideration of the Classical system. In equation (3.40), the supply of labor has been assumed to depend on the real wage, i.e. the money wage divided by the price index. A devaluation raises the price index, and, therefore, is equivalent to a drop in the real wage, given the money wage. This, in turn, means that less labor services will be supplied at the old money wage rate.[23] From equation (3.39) it is apparent that the demand for labor depends on the money wage rate and the price of the domestic good. If both the labor demand and labor supply curves are graphed in the $(w/p, N)$ plane, this means that, from the point of view of producers, the labor supply curve has shifted to the left, as in Figure 3.6. Of course, in the normal

---

[23] Differentiation of the labor supply function yields $\partial N^s / \partial e = -(1 - \alpha)w N^s_{w/\Phi} < 0$.

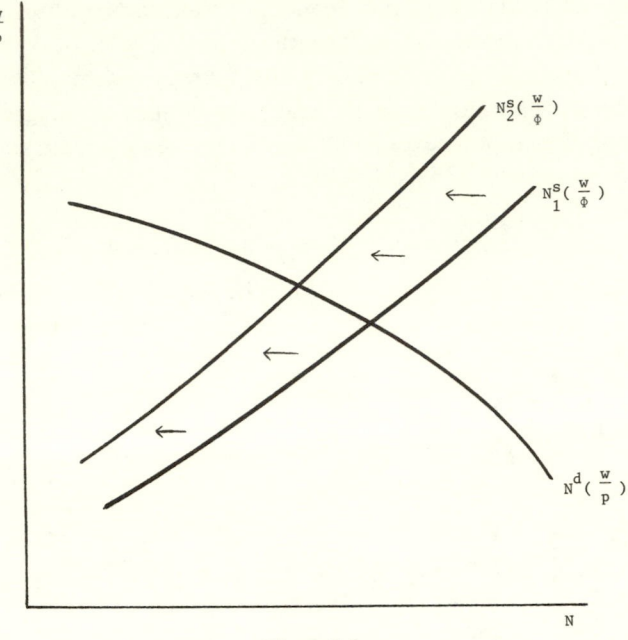

Figure 3.6

case, the devaluation also will shift the aggregate demand curve. Thus, the final effect of the devaluation on the level of employment will depend on the net effect of the shifts of the two curves.

To determine this net effect note that, since the production function is monotonically increasing in the labor argument, determining the change in the equilibrium level of output is equivalent to determining the change in employment. The use of Cramer's Rule to solve the system of total differentials of equations (3.1) through (3.10) and (3.39) through (3.42) for dY/de results in

$$(3.45) \qquad \frac{dY}{de} = -\frac{m}{\Delta_5} \frac{D_i}{L_i},$$

84

where $\Delta_5 = 1 - D_y - \theta(X_{p/e} - D_{eq}) + (D_i/L_i)[L_{\bar{Y}} + \theta(\alpha m + (1 - \alpha)yL_{\bar{Y}})]$, and where $\theta =$ the reciprocal of the right-hand side of equation (3.43). Since $\theta > 0$, given all earlier assumptions $\Delta_5 > 0$. This gives the somewhat surprising result that dY/de will unambiguously fall with a devaluation.

Fortunately, equation (3.45) makes clear the source of this result. In the closed-economy model, with perfectly flexible prices and wages, all real effects are independent of the monetary sector. Any money price change that caused the labor supply function to shift would be exactly offset by price changes causing the labor demand function to shift by the same amount. In an open-economy system, it is possible to change a "real" variable (the real wage) by means of a change in a monetary variable (the exchange rate). As other monetary prices attempt to respond to this change, thus generating an offsetting shift of the demand curve, the fact that the stock of nominal money is fixed causes the interest rate to rise since the real value of the stock falls. This lowers the domestic demand curve for goods, and keeps the aggregate demand curve, and hence the labor demand curve, from shifting by an equal offsetting amount. The result is a drop in output and employment.

This result also holds for the absorption function specification of the model. In this case, equation (3.45) becomes

$$(3.46) \qquad \frac{dY}{de} = - \frac{m}{\Delta_6} \frac{\bar{A}_i - F_i}{L_i}$$

where $\Delta_6 = h + f - \theta X(1 + \eta_X + \eta_F - h) + [(\bar{A}_i - F_i)/L_i][L_{\bar{Y}} + \theta(\alpha m + (1 - \alpha)yL_{\bar{Y}})]$. Since $\bar{A}_i - F_i < 0$ whenever $D_i < 0$,[24] if $dY^d/dp < 0$, then $\Delta_6 > 0$ and $dY/de < 0$.

Balance of Payments Effects

Although the effect of a devaluation on the level of employment and output is unambiguous, it turns out that its effect on the

---

[24] See footnote 14.

balance of trade will depend on the Marshall-Lerner condition. Solving the complete Classical system (equations (3.1) through (3.10) and (3.39) through (3.42)) for dB/de by means of Cramer's Rule gives

$$(3.47) \qquad \frac{dB}{de} = \frac{m}{\Delta_5} \left\{ \frac{F_i}{L_i} [1 - D_y - \theta(X_{p/e} - D_{eq})] \right.$$
$$\left. + \frac{D_i}{L_i} [F_y - \theta X(1 + \eta_X + \eta_F)] \right\}.$$

If it is assumed that the aggregate demand curve is negatively sloped, then $dB/de > 0$ if $(1 + \eta_X + \eta_F) < 0$, i.e. if the simple Marshall-Lerner condition holds.[25] In a world of flexible prices and money wages, and a Classical labor supply function, therefore, the traditional Marshall-Lerner condition is sufficient to guarantee that the trade balance will improve with a devaluation. However, as in the Keynesian case, it is not a necessary condition. If it does not hold (i.e. if $(1 + \eta_X + \eta_F) > 0$) then $dB/de \gtreqless 0$ as

$$(3.48) \qquad \left| \frac{F_i}{L_i} [1 - D_y - \theta(X_{p/e} - D_{eq})] + \frac{D_i}{L_i} F_y \right|$$
$$\gtreqless \left| \theta \frac{D_i}{L_i} X(1 + \eta_X + \eta_F) \right|.$$

The equivalent result for the absorption function version of the model is

$$(3.49) \qquad \frac{dB}{de} = \frac{m}{\Delta_6} \left\{ \frac{F_i}{L_i} h(1 + \theta X) \right.$$
$$\left. + \frac{\overline{A}_i}{L_i} [f - \theta X(1 + \eta_X + \eta_F)] \right\}.$$

---

[25] It is of some interest to note that, in this case, the simple Marshall-Lerner condition has a role to play only if supply functions are *not* infinitely elastic. This is in contrast to the standard elasticities approach, where the simple Marshall-Lerner condition emerges only if export supply functions are infinitely elastic.

Again, if the Marshall-Lerner condition is met, then $dB/de > 0$. If it is not, then $dB/de > 0$ if

$$(3.50) \qquad \left| \frac{F_i}{L_i} h(1 + \theta X) + \bar{A}_i f \right| > \left| \frac{A_i}{L_i} \theta X(1 + \eta_X + \eta_F) \right|.$$

It is interesting to note that if there are no interest rate effects in this system (or, alternatively, if the Classical monetary authorities follow a Keynesian neutral monetary policy) then a devaluation has no effect on the balance of payments or on the level of employment. In this case $F_i = D_i = \bar{A}_i = 0$ (and/ or $L_i \to \infty$), and a glance at equations (3.45) through (3.49) reveals that $dY/de = dB/de = 0$. Of course, this is exactly what a Classical economist would expect, since with flexible prices and wages and no effects from changes in the real value of the money supply (or no change in the real money supply), no underlying real variables have been affected by the change in the exchange rate.

IV A STABILITY ANALYSIS OF THE MODEL

One popular exercise in studies of this sort is to use an analysis of the stability properties of the system via the Correspondence Principle to provide additional restrictions on the various parameters of the model, and to supply at least one test of its internal consistency. In many cases this exercise has the effect either of making determinate results that otherwise would be ambiguous or of revealing as economically absurd some of the tentative conclusions reached in the comparative statics analysis. In other cases, however, it is so poorly applied that it generates statements that, if not incorrect, are at least very misleading.

This section presents a stability analysis of the basic model developed above. This analysis indicates that an overly strong condition sufficient to guarantee local stability of the model with the adjustment mechanism specified here is that the demand curve for domestically produced goods always have a negative slope. This conclusion is the principal justification for assuming that $dY^d/dP < 0$. In addition, the method used to obtain this stability condition is used to show the riskiness inherent in Correspondence Principle analysis. It also shows, by implication, that the long-accepted conclusion of Tsiang—that Keynesian neutral monetary policy is unstable—is not necessarily true.

Correspondence Principle Analysis

Before specifying a dynamic adjustment mechanism and undertaking a stability analysis, this section will briefly review the general nature of Correspondence Principle analysis. While it has been more than twenty-five years since Samuelson first set out his now famous Correspondence Principle in the *Foundations of Economic Analysis*, it is apparent from the literature that some perspective is necessary.

The important point to be made here is that there is no such thing as *the* stability analysis of a model, or *the* stability condition or set of conditions, when the Correspondence Principle is employed. This follows from the basic nature of the technique. As is well known, the method of analysis in comparative statics is to define a system of equations for which an equilibrium state exists, or is assumed to exist, then to compare this equilibrium with an alternate one which would exist if a control variable were changed. Since nothing is said or implied about the path taken by the economy as it moves between the two equilibria, to look at the question of stability (i.e. will the economy in fact adjust so as to reach—or at least tend to converge toward—a new equilibrium after being displaced from the old one) requires the specification of a new model that sets out the adjustment mechanism assumed to be operating.

It should be clear that, in principle at least, any number of dynamic adjustment mechanisms consistent with the static model under consideration could be specified. While potential adjustment processes may prove to be unreasonable by virtue of the economic behavior they imply, it is not true in general that there will be only one plausible dynamic adjustment process. This, in turn, suggests that any appeal to the Correspondence Principle ought to include an explicit statement of the adjustment process being assumed, in order to allow the reader to make his own judgment about the reasonableness of the dynamic mechanism assumed. This is especially significant when the conclusion of some analysis is that policy X is more (less) desirable because it improves (weakens) the probability of the adjustment process's being "stable."

Stability of the Basic Model

The aggregate-supply–aggregate-demand framework within which the macroeconomic model was developed is particularly useful when a dynamic adjustment specification is being sought because it suggests the standard general equilibrium approach of making changes in price a positive function of the level of excess demand. Thus,

$$(3.51) \qquad \dot{p} = \Pi(Y^d - Y^s); \qquad \Pi' > 0,$$

where, as usual, dotted variables denote time derivatives. Equilibrium implies that both excess demand and the rate of change of prices be zero, so that $\Pi(0) = 0$. Since both the exchange rate and money supply are fixed, both Y^d and Y^s are functions only of p, and equation (3.51) can be written as

$$(3.52) \qquad \dot{p} = \Pi[Y^d(p) - Y^s(p)].$$

Use of a Taylor's series expansion to provide a linear approximation of equation (3.52) around the equilibrium price yields

(3.53) $\dot{p} = \Pi[Y^d(p^*) - Y^s(p^*)]$

$+ \Pi' \cdot [(Y_p^d - Y_p^s)(p - p^*)]$,

where an asterisk is used to denote the equilibrium value of a variable. Subscripts still denote derivatives, so that $Y_p^d = \partial Y^d/\partial p$. Since in equilibrium $Y^d = Y^s$, equation (3.53) becomes

(3.54) $\dot{p} = \Pi(0) + \Pi' \cdot (Y_p^d - Y_p^s)(p - p^*)$

$= \Pi' \cdot (Y_p^d - Y_p^s)(p - p^*)$.

Since equation (3.54) is a nonhomogeneous first-order differential equation, by inspection it yields the solution

(3.55) $p(t) = [p(0) - p^*]e^{\Pi' \cdot (Y_p^d - Y_p^s)t} + p^*$.

In this context, stability requires that, if $p(t) \neq p^*$, then $p(t) \rightarrow p^*$ as $t \rightarrow \infty$. This latter condition requires, in turn, that the first term of equation (3.55) vanish as $t \rightarrow \infty$. Since $\Pi' > 0$, this is equivalent to requiring that $(Y_p^d - Y_p^s) < 0$. Explicitly substituting for Y_p^d and Y_p^d from equations (3.12) and (2.17) in the Keynesian case yields

(3.56) $Y_p^d - Y_p^s = \dfrac{1}{\Delta_1}\left[X_{p/e} - D_{eq} \right.$

$\left. - \dfrac{D_i}{L_i}(\alpha m + (1 - \alpha)yL_{\bar{y}}) \right] - \dfrac{1}{\beta}$.

Since Δ_1 and $\beta > 0$, a sufficient condition to guarantee stability in this case is to assume that $Y_p^d < 0$, so that $[X_{p/e} - D_{eq} - (D_i/L_i)(\alpha m + (1 - \alpha)yL_{\bar{y}})] < 0$. If $D_i = 0$ or $L_i \rightarrow \infty$, then a sufficient condition to insure stability is $X_{p/e} - D_{eq} < 0$. It is of some interest to note that gross substitutability between all goods, which is sufficient to guarantee stability in Walrasian barter models, also guarantees stability here.[26]

[26] The Classical case yields the similar condition that the model is stable if $X_{p/e} - D_{eq} - (D_i/L_i)(\alpha m + (1 - \alpha)yL_{\bar{y}}) - \theta < 0$.

Alternate Approaches to Stability

From the discussion above, it should be clear that this stability condition depends crucially on the adjustment mechanism specified. A particularly graphic way to see the difference the adjustment mechanism chosen makes in the analysis is to consider an alternate specification. The condition obtained above is based on the implicit assumption that the money market, which was solved out of the system as part of the aggregate demand curve, adjusts at the same rate as the goods market. An equally plausible alternative is to assume that the money market adjusts instantaneously, or at least so much quicker than the goods market that it can be considered to be always in equilibrium. This assumption originally was advanced by Samuelson (1965), and is the standard assumption in textbook discussions of the stability of the IS-LM model.[27]

If it is assumed that the rate of change of prices depends on the excess demand in the goods market, the dynamic model is

(3.57)
$$\dot{p} = \Pi[Y^d(p, i) - Y^s(p)]$$
$$0 = L(\bar{Y}, i) - \frac{m}{\Phi},$$

where now Y^d is a function of p and i because the interest rate has not been solved out of the system.

By using a Taylor's series expansion to obtain a linear approximation to equations (3.57) in the neighborhood of the equilibrium p and i, the model becomes

(3.58)
$$\dot{p} = \left(\frac{\partial Y^d}{\partial p} - \frac{\partial Y^s}{\partial p}\right)(p - p^*) + \frac{\partial Y^d}{\partial i}(i - i^*)$$
$$0 = \left(\frac{\partial L}{\partial p} - \frac{\partial(m/\Phi)}{\partial p}\right)(p - p^*) + \frac{\partial L}{\partial i}(i - i^*).$$

---

[27] This assumption generates the stability requirement cited in Chapter 2 (page 38).

Solving for the various partial derivatives and substituting into equations (3.58) results in

$$\dot{p} = \frac{\beta(X_{p/e} - D_{eq}) - (1 - D_y)}{\beta(1 - D_y)}(p - p^*)$$

$$+ \frac{D_i}{(1 - D_y)}(i - i^*)$$

(3.59)

$$0 = \frac{L_{\bar{Y}} + \beta(\alpha m + (1 - \alpha)yL_{\bar{Y}})}{\beta}(p - p^*)$$

$$+ L_i(i - i^*).$$

Denoting the characteristic root of the single differential equation by λ, the characteristic determinant is

$$\begin{vmatrix} \dfrac{\beta(X_{p/e} - D_{eq}) - (1 - D_y)}{\beta(1 - D_y)} - \lambda & \dfrac{D_i}{1 - D_y} \\[2ex] \dfrac{L_{\bar{Y}} + \beta(\alpha m + (1 - \alpha)yL_{\bar{Y}})}{\beta} & L_i \end{vmatrix}.$$

Solving this for λ and recalling that stability requires that the characteristic root be negative, yields the condition that the model is stable if

(3.60) $1 - D_y - \beta(X_{p/e} - D_{eq})$

$$+ \frac{D_i}{L_i}[L_{\bar{Y}} + \beta(\alpha m + (1 - \alpha)yL_{\bar{Y}})] > 0,$$

or, stability requires (in this case) that $\Delta_3 > 0$.

As this alternate approach indicates, it is possible to obtain a different stability condition if the specification of the dynamic adjustment mechanism is changed. Clearly, if the assumption that the money market were to adjust instantaneously were relaxed, and an additional differential equation introduced into the system, a different set of conditions would emerge. This is pointed out because Tsiang (1961) has asserted, without specifying an adjustment mechanism, that Keynesian neutral

92

monetary policy guarantees instability as the economy approaches full employment. However, in the absence of an explicit adjustment mechanism, this statement is clearly not correct. Even if there is some adjustment mechanism for which it is true, in general there will exist others for which it is not. For example, if it is assumed that, at full employment, the economy behaves in the same manner as the Classical system described above, then Keynesian neutral monetary policy does not induce instability.

This becomes more clear if the most extreme case possible is considered. Assume that the labor supply curve is perfectly inelastic, so that no changes in aggregate output can occur (i.e. $N^s_{w/\Phi} = 0$, so that $dY^s = 0$). If the monetary authorities peg the interest rate, so that $di = 0$, then equations (3.57) become (effectively)

(3.61)
$$\dot{p} = \Pi[Y^d(p) - Y^s(p)]$$
$$0 = L(\bar{Y}) - \frac{m}{\Phi}.$$

Again using a Taylor's series expansion to provide a linear approximation of equations (3.61) in the neighborhood of equilibrium, and recalling that a Keynesian neutral monetary policy implies that the money supply is an endogenous variable, yields

(3.62)
$$\dot{p} = \frac{\partial Y^d}{\partial p}(p - p^*)$$
$$0 = \left(\frac{\partial L}{\partial p} - \frac{\partial(m/\Phi)}{\partial p}\right)(p - p^*) - \frac{\partial(m/\Phi)}{\partial m}(m - m^*).$$

or,

(3.63)
$$\dot{p} = \left[\frac{X_{p/e} - D_{eq}}{1 - D_y}\right](p - p^*)$$
$$0 = [\alpha m + (1 - \alpha)yL_{\bar{Y}}](p - p^*) - \frac{1}{\Phi}(m - m^*).$$

In this case, the characteristic determinant is

$$\begin{vmatrix} \dfrac{X_{p/e} - D_{eq}}{1 - D_y} - \lambda & 0 \\[2ex] \alpha m + (1 - \alpha)yL_{\bar{Y}} & -\dfrac{1}{\Phi} \end{vmatrix}$$

Since stability requires that $\lambda < 0$, the model is stable if $X_{p/e} - D_{eq} < 0$. Clearly, gross substitutability will insure that the system is stable.

Appendix A: Mathematical Derivations

THE principal equations and results of the aggregate model developed and used in the chapter are presented here. Since the Keynesian and Classical cases differ only in the specification of the labor market, they are developed together. All results are derived only for the separate demand functions versions of the model. To convert any results to the equivalent aggregate expenditure function version, use should be made of equation (3.22), which is derived in the text.[1]

I THE BASIC COMPONENTS OF THE MODEL

Aggregate Demand

The demand side of the model is identical in both the Keynesian and Classical cases, and is determined from equations (3.1) through (3.10). Since some common equilibrium conditions were taken for granted when those equations were listed, the complete set of equations—four behavioral, seven definitional, and one equilibrium condition—is set out here. Using the notation defined in the chapter, these equations are:

Behavioral Equations:

(3A.1)　　$D = D(y, p, eq, i)$;
$$0 < D_y < 1, D_p < 0, D_{eq} = ?, D_i < 0,$$

(3A.2)　　$F = F(y, p, eq, i)$;
$$0 < F_y < 1, F_p = ?, F_{eq} < 0, F_i < 0,$$

(3A.3)　　$X = X(p/e)$;　$X_{p/e} < 0$,

(3A.4)　　$L = L(\bar{Y}, i.)$;　$L_{\bar{Y}} > 0, L_i < 0$.

---

[1] It should be noted explicitly that all results are valid only as local approximations around the point where $B = 0$.

95

Definitional Equations:

(3A.5) $Y = \dfrac{A}{p} + \dfrac{B}{p}$,

(3A.6) $A = pD + eqF$,

(3A.7) $B = pX - eqF$,

(3A.8) $\dfrac{m}{\Phi} = M =$ real money supply,

(3A.9) $y = pY$,

(3A.10) $\bar{Y} = \dfrac{y}{\Phi}$,

(3A.11) $\Phi = \alpha p + (1 - \alpha)\, eq$.

Equilibrium Condition:

(3A.12) $M = L$.

In the text, equation (3A.12) was (implicitly) assumed to hold, and equations (3A.4), (3A.8), and (3A.12) were combined as

(3A.13) $M = \dfrac{m}{\Phi} = L(\bar{Y}, i)$.

Aggregate demand for the domestically produced good can be obtained by first substituting equations (3A.6) and (3A.7) into (3A.5) to get

(3A.5a) $Y = D + X$,

and observing that, since F does not appear in the definition of Y, substitution of equations (3A.1), (3A.2), (3A.3), and (3A.9) through (3A.11) into equation 3A.5a) yields a single equation giving Y as a function of p, m, and e;

(3A.14) $Y^d = Y^d(p, m, e)$.

Equation (3A.14) was referred to as the aggregate demand

equation. To obtain dY^d/dp, dY^d/de, and dY^d/dm, totally differentiate equations (3A.1), (3A.3), (3A.5a), (3A.9) through (3A.11), and (3A.13), and substitute the differentiated versions of (3A.1), (3A.3), and (3A.9) through (3A.11) into the differentiated versions of equations (3A.5a) and (3A.13). Since units were initially chosen so that $p = q = e = 1$, it follows that $\Phi = 1$ and $y = Y = \bar{Y}$. Making use of these two facts yields

$$(3A.15) \qquad dY^d = D_y \, dY^d + (D_p + yD_y + X_{p/e}) \, dp$$
$$+ (D_{eq} - X_{p/e}) \, de + D_i \, di,$$

and

$$(3A.16) \qquad dm = L_{\bar{Y}} \, dY^d + [\alpha m + (1 - \alpha)yL_{\bar{Y}}] \, dp$$
$$+ [(1 - \alpha)(m - yL_{\bar{Y}})] \, de + L_i \, di.$$

The assumption that demand functions are zero-degree homogeneous in p, eq, and y implies that $D_p + D_{eq} + yD_y = F_p + F_{eq} + yF_y = 0$. Solving equation (3A.16) for di, substituting this into (3A.15), and making use of the homogeneity property yields

$$(3A.17) \qquad dY^d = \frac{1}{\Delta_1} \left\{ \left[X_{p/e} - D_{eq} \right. \right.$$
$$\left. - \frac{D_i}{L_i}(\alpha m + (1 - \alpha)yL_{\bar{Y}}) \right] dp + \frac{D_i}{L_i} dm$$
$$\left. - \left[X_{p/e} - D_{eq} + \frac{D_i}{L_i}(1 - \alpha)(m - yL_{\bar{Y}}) \right] de \right\},$$

where $\Delta_1 = 1 - D_y + (D_i/L_i)L_{\bar{Y}}$. Equation (3.12) and, in the next chapter, equations (4.12) and (4.14) are obtained directly from equation (3A.17).

Short-Run Balance of Payments Equilibrium Line

The locus of points for which trade is balanced in the short run is found from a second subset of the demand equations.

By setting $B = 0$ in equation (3A.7), then substituting in from equations (3A.2), (3A.3), (3A.13), and (3A.9) through (3A.11), a single implicit function in Y, p, m, and e is obtained. If the conditions of the implicit function theorem are met, this can be solved to yield

$$(3A.18) \qquad Y^B = Y^B(p, m, e).$$

For specified values of p, m, and e, equation (3A.18) gives the value of Y for which trade is balanced. To obtain the total differential of equation (3A.18), totally differentiate equations (3A.7) (setting $dB = 0$), (3A.2), (3A.3), and (3A.9), and solve for dY^B to get

$$(3A.19) \qquad dY^B = \frac{1}{F_y} \{(X_{p/e} + X - F_p - yF_p)\, dp$$
$$- (X_{p/e} + F_{eq} + F)\, de - F_i\, di\}.$$

Solving equation (3A.16) for di, substituting into (3A.19), and making use of the homogeneity properties of the demand functions, and the facts that, since $B = 0$ and $p = e = q = \Phi = 1$, $X = F$ yields

$$(3A.20) \qquad dY^B = \frac{1}{\Delta_2} \left\{ \left[X(1 + \eta_X + \eta_F) \right. \right.$$
$$\left. + \frac{F_i}{L_i}(\alpha m + (1 - \alpha)yL_{\bar{Y}}) \right] dp$$
$$- \frac{F_i}{L_i}\, dm - \left[X(1 + \eta_X + \eta_F) \right.$$
$$\left. \left. - \frac{F_i}{L_i}(1 - \alpha)(m - yL_{\bar{Y}}) \right] de \right\},$$

where $\Delta_2 = F_y - (F_i/L_i)L_{\bar{Y}}$.

Equation (3A.20) yields equations (3.18) and (later) (4.13) and (4.15).

Aggregate Supply

The different specifications of the labor market in the Keynesian and Classical cases imply that the aggregate supply side of the model will differ in the two versions. In the Keynesian analysis, labor supply is assumed to be infinitely elastic at the prevailing money wage rate, which is equivalent to saying that the level of employment is demand determined. Thus, the Keynesian aggregate supply function is determined from: (1) an aggregate production function,

$$(3A.21) \qquad Y = Y(N),$$

which is a function only of the quantity of labor employed since the capital stock is fixed; (2) a labor demand function (or, equivalently, a function setting the money wage rate equal to the value of the marginal product of labor),

$$(3A.22) \qquad w = pY_N(N),$$

and (3) a definition fixing the money wage rate,

$$(3A.23) \qquad w = \bar{w} \text{ (for } N \leq N^*).$$

These three equations reduce to a single function in Y and p, or

$$(3A.24) \qquad Y^s = Y^s(p).$$

Totally differentiating equations (3A.21) through (3A.23) and solving for dY^s yields the total differential of equation (3A.24), or

$$(3A.25) \qquad dY^S = -\frac{Y_N^2}{Y_{NN}} dp,$$

or, since $\beta = -(Y_{NN}/Y_N^2)$

$$(3A.25a) \qquad dY = \frac{1}{\beta} dp.$$

In the Classical case, aggregate supply is determined from (1) equation (3A.21), (2) a labor demand function,

$$(3A.26) \qquad N^d = N^d\left(\frac{w}{p}\right); \quad N^d_{w/p} < 0,$$

(3) a labor supply function,

$$(3A.27) \qquad N^s = N^s\left(\frac{w}{\Phi}\right); \quad N^s_{w/\Phi} > 0,$$

(4) the equilibrium condition that labor demand equal labor supply,

$$(3A.28) \qquad N^d = N^s,$$

and (5) equation (3A.11). These five equations reduce to

$$(3A.29) \qquad Y^s = Y^s(p, e).$$

The total differential of this equation can be found by differentiating the four underlying equations and solving for dY^s. This yields

$$(3A.30) \qquad dY^s = \hat{\theta}\, dp - \hat{\theta}\, de$$

where $\hat{\theta} = (1 - \alpha)w Y_N N^d_{w/p}(N^s_{w/\Phi}/N^d_{w/p} - N^s_{w/\Phi})$.

II THE COMPLETE MODELS IN THE SMALL-COUNTRY CASE

Keynesian Model

The basic structure of the complete Keynesian model may be found by taking the totally differentiated versions of equations (3A.1) through (3A.12) and equation (3A.25a) and reducing them to three equations in the endogenous variables dY, di, and dB (or, equivalently, in dY, dp, and $dB)^2$ and the control

---

[2] As it turns out, it is easiest to solve for dB/de and dB/dm if dp is solved out of the system, while dY/de and dY/dm are found most readily if di is solved out. Obviously, either approach yields exactly the same results.

variables de and dm. Since $B = 0$, $p = e = q = \Phi = 1$, and $X = F$, this system can be expressed as

$$(3A.31) \quad \begin{bmatrix} 1 - D_y + \beta(D_{eq} - X_{p/e}) & -D_i & 0 \\ F_y - \beta(F_{eq} + X_{p/e} + X) & F_i & 1 \\ L_{\bar{Y}} + \beta(\alpha m + (1 - \alpha)yL_{\bar{Y}}) & L_i & 0 \end{bmatrix} \begin{bmatrix} dY \\ di \\ dB \end{bmatrix}$$

$$= \begin{bmatrix} D_{eq} - X_{p/e} & 0 \\ -(X_{p/e} + F_{eq} + F) & 0 \\ -(1 - \alpha)(m - yL_{\bar{Y}}) & 1 \end{bmatrix} \begin{bmatrix} de \\ dm \end{bmatrix}.$$

The determinant of the coefficient matrix of equations (3A.31) is

$$\Delta = -\{L_i[1 - D_y + \beta(D_{eq} - X_{p/e})] + D_i[L_{\bar{Y}} + \beta(\alpha m + (1 - \alpha)yL_{\bar{Y}})]\},$$

$\Delta > 0$ if $(D_{eq} - X_{p/e}) > 0$. This is assured if it is assumed that $dY^d/dp < 0$ always, including the case where interest rate effects are zero, or if it is assumed that the model is stable as discussed in the text. This determinant becomes Δ_3 by virtue of the fact that, when Cramer's Rule is used to solve for the various effects of a change in a control variable, the numerator and denominator of the resulting expressions have been multiplied by $1/L_i$.

Equations (3.23), (3.33), and (later) (4.3) can be obtained by applying Cramer's Rule to equations (3A.31). In each case, to obtain the final equation use must be made of the homogeneity properties of the demand functions, the fact that $B = 0$, and a considerable amount of tedious algebraic manipulation.

Classical Model

The complete Classical system can be found by taking equations (3A.1) through (3A.12) along with equation (3A.30), totally differentiating them and solving down to three equations in dY, di (or dp), and dB and the controls de and dm.

Only the aggregate supply side of the model is changed between the Keynesian and Classical cases, however this yields a three equation Classical system of the form

$$(3A.32) \quad \begin{bmatrix} 1 - D_y + \theta(D_{eq} - X_{p/e}) & -D_i & 0 \\ F_y - \theta(X_{p/e} + F_{eq} + F) & F_i & 1 \\ L_{\bar{Y}} + \theta(\alpha m + (1 - \alpha)yL_{\bar{Y}}) & L_i & 0 \end{bmatrix} \begin{bmatrix} dY \\ di \\ dB \end{bmatrix}$$

$$= \begin{bmatrix} 0 & 0 \\ 0 & 0 \\ -m & 1 \end{bmatrix} \begin{bmatrix} de \\ dm \end{bmatrix}$$

and where $\theta = 1/\hat{\theta}$.

The coefficient matrix on the left-hand side of equations (A3.32) differs from that of equations (A3.31) only by the difference in magnitude between θ and β, which means that, qualitatively, the determinant of this matrix is the same as the determinant for equations (3A.31). Replacing β with θ in the determinant of the Keynesian system yields the determinant of the Classical system.

Equations (3.45), (3.47), and in Chapter 4, (4.8) and (4.26), can be found by using Cramer's Rule on equations (3A.32). As a comparison of the coefficient matrices on the left-hand side of the two systems makes obvious, changes in the money supply have qualitatively the same results in both worlds, while changes in the exchange rate do not. This difference follows from the differing structure in the aggregate supply side of the two systems.

Appendix B: A Two-Country Model

IN light of the complexities of the model developed here, and in order to highlight its new features, it was useful to concentrate on the small-country version of the model. Conceptually, however, extension of the model from the small-country case to the more general two-country case is straightforward. In this appendix, the basic structure of such a two-country model is outlined for both the Keynesian and Classical versions of the model. Since the qualitative conclusions reached in the text are not altered by the extension to two countries, while the algebraic complexity and intuitive interpretation of the model both become more difficult, especially in the Keynesian system, only some illustrative special cases are explicitly solved here.

I THE KEYNESIAN VERSION OF THE MODEL

In extending the Keynesian system to the two-country case, equation (3A.3) must be modified to be

$$(3B.1) \qquad X = X\left(y^*, \frac{p}{e}, q, i^*\right); \qquad X_{y^*} > 0,$$

$$X_{p/e} < 0, X_q = ?, X_{i^*} < 0,$$

and where asterisks are used to denote foreign country variables. In addition, a complete set of equations describing the foreign country must be specified. Analogous to the small-country case, these are

$$(3B.2) \qquad D^* = D^*\left(y^*, \frac{p}{e}, q, i^*\right); \qquad 0 < D_y^* < 1,$$

$$D_{p/e}^* = ?, D_q^* < 0, D_i^* < 0,$$

$$(3B.3) \qquad L^* = L^*(\bar{Y}^*, i^*); \qquad L_{\bar{Y}}^* > 0, L_i^* < 0,$$

$$(3B.4) \qquad Y^* = \left(A^* - \frac{B}{e}\right)\Big/ q,$$

$$(3B.5) \qquad A^* = qD^* + \frac{p}{e}X^*,$$

$$(3B.6) \qquad \left(\frac{m}{\Phi}\right)^* = M^* = \text{foreign real money supply},$$

$$(3B.7) \qquad y^* = qY^*,$$

$$(3B.8) \qquad \bar{Y} = \frac{y^*}{\Phi^*},$$

$$(3B.9) \qquad \Phi^* = (1 - \gamma)\frac{p}{e} + \gamma q,$$

$$(3B.10) \qquad M^* = L^*,$$

and a supply equation

$$(3B.11) \qquad Y^{*s} = Y^{*s}(q), \text{ where } dY^* = \frac{1}{\beta^*}dq.$$

Differentiating the complete two-country model, and reducing it to a five-equation system in the five endogenous variables dY, dY^*, di, di^*, and dB, and the three exogenous variables dm, dm^*, and de results in

(3B.12)

$$\begin{bmatrix} 1 - D_y + \beta(D_{eq} - X_{p/e}) & -D_i & 0 & -X_i^* & -[X_y^* + \beta^*(D_{eq} - X_{p/e})] \\ F_y + \beta(D_{p/e}^* - F_{eq}) & F_i & 0 & D_i^* & -[1 - D_y^* + \beta^*(D_{p/e}^* - F_{eq})] \\ F_y - \beta X(1 + \eta_X + \eta_F) & F_i & 1 & -X_i^* & -[X_y^* - \beta^* X(1 + \eta_X + \eta_F)] \\ L_{\bar{Y}} + \beta(\alpha m + (1 - \alpha)yL_{\bar{Y}}) & L_i & 0 & 0 & \beta^*(1 - \alpha)(m - yL_{\bar{Y}}) \\ \beta(1 - \gamma)(m^* - y^* L_{\bar{Y}}^*) & 0 & 0 & L_i^* & L_{\bar{Y}}^* + \beta^*(\gamma m^* + (1 - \gamma)y^* L_{\bar{Y}}^*) \end{bmatrix} \begin{bmatrix} dY \\ di \\ dB \\ di^* \\ dY^* \end{bmatrix}$$

$$= \begin{bmatrix} 0 & 0 & D_{eq} - X_{p/e} \\ 0 & 0 & D_{p/e}^* - F_{eq} \\ 0 & 0 & -X(1 + \eta_X + \eta_F) \\ 1 & 0 & -(1 - \alpha)(m - yL_{\bar{Y}}) \\ 0 & 1 & (1 - \gamma)(m^* - y^* L_{\bar{Y}}^*) \end{bmatrix} \begin{bmatrix} dm \\ dm^* \\ de \end{bmatrix}.$$

Observe that asterisks have been dropped from subscripts in equation (3B.12), where interpretation should be obvious.

As is readily apparent from equation (3B.12), completely general expressions for dY/de, dY^*/de, dB/de, etc., are quite complex. Moreover, as was noted above, solving for them does not alter the general qualitative conclusions reached in the chapter, although intuitive explanations of the results are hard to provide. However, to indicate the throughly general nature of the model, it is interesting to examine some special cases.

If it is assumed that supply curves in both countries are infinitely elastic, so that $\beta = \beta^* = 0$, and that interest rate changes do not affect the demand for goods, then solving for the effect of a change in the exchange rate yields

$$(3B.13) \qquad \frac{dB}{de} = \frac{1}{\Delta} \{[(1 - D_y)(1 - D_y^*) - F_y X_y^*]$$

$$\times [X(1 + \eta_X + \eta_F)]$$

$$- X_y^*(D_{p/e}^* - F_{eq})(1 - D_y - F_y)$$

$$- F_y(D_{eq} - X_{p/e})(1 - D_y^* - X_y^*)\},$$

where $\Delta = (1 - D_y)(1 - D_y^*) - F_y X_y^*$. Since $1 - D_y - F_y > 0$, $1 - D_y > F_y$, and likewise for the foreign country. Therefore, $\Delta > 0$, and $dB/de > 0$ if all goods are gross substitutes in each country and the simple Marshall-Lerner condition is met.

A more interesting result emerges if equation (3.22) is used to convert equation (3B.13) to an aggregate expenditure framework. In this case, dB/de becomes

$$(3B.13a) \qquad \frac{dB}{de} = \frac{hh^* X[1 + \eta_X + \eta_F + f + f^*]}{hh^* + hf^* + h^*f},$$

which is immediately recognizable as Harberger's result. That the introduction of money greatly complicates the analysis can be readily seen if the assumption of infinitely elastic supply curves is retained while interest rate changes are allowed to affect demand for commodities. In this case, the effect of a devaluation on the balance of trade in the aggregate expenditure function version of the model is given by

$$(3B.14) \quad \frac{dB}{de} = \frac{1}{\Delta_{3B}} \{X[(L_{\bar{Y}}(\bar{A}_i(1 + \eta_X + \eta_F) - F_ih)$$

$$+ L_ih(1 + \eta_X + \eta_F + f))(L_{\bar{Y}}^*\bar{A}_i^* + L_i^*h^*)$$

$$+ h^*(L_{\bar{Y}}\bar{A}_i + L_ih)(L_i^*f^* - L_{\bar{Y}}^*X_i)]$$

$$- (1 - \alpha)(1 - \mu)m(L_{\bar{Y}}^*\bar{A}_i^* + L_i^*h^*)(\bar{A}_if + F_ih)$$

$$+ (1 - \gamma)(1 - \mu^*)m^*(L_{\bar{Y}}\bar{A}_i + L_ih)(\bar{A}_i^*f^* + X_ih^*)\},$$

where $\Delta_{3B} = -\{L_i^*[L_{\bar{Y}}(\bar{A}_i(h^* + f^*) - F_ih^*)$

$$+ L_i(hh^* + h^*f + hf^*)]$$

$$+ L_{\bar{Y}}^*[L_{\bar{Y}}(\bar{A}_i(A_i^* - X_i)$$

$$- F_i\bar{A}_i^*) + L_i(h(\bar{A}_i - X_i) + fX_i)].$$

Obviously, the introduction of interest rate effects greatly complicates the effects of a devaluation on the short-run balance of trade. In addition to considering the effects of the exchange rate change on the real value of the domestic money supply, there are also parallel effects in the foreign money supply, as well as direct price effects and income effects that all influence the final result.[1]

II A CLASSICAL WORLD

In light of the complexities revealed by such results as equation (3B.14) the analytic appeal of a Classical environment, where the homogeneity properties of the various functions impose a regularity missing in a Keynesian world, is more than obvious. As in the small-country case, the demand side

---

[1] Conditions for $dB/de > 0$ can be easily worked out by the reader.

of the model carries over from the Keynesian to the Classical system, while the supply equations in both countries must be modified to incorporate Classical labor market conditions. When this is done, and the system differentiated and reduced to a system of five equations in the endogenous variables dY, dY^*, di, di^*, and dB, and the control variables dm, dm^*, and de, the result is

$$
(3B.15) \qquad [A] \begin{bmatrix} dY \\ di \\ dB \\ di^* \\ dY^* \end{bmatrix} = \begin{bmatrix} 0 & 0 & 0 \\ 0 & 0 & 0 \\ 0 & 0 & 0 \\ 1 & 0 & -m \\ 0 & 1 & m^* \end{bmatrix} \begin{bmatrix} dm \\ dm^* \\ de \end{bmatrix},
$$

where the coefficient matrix A is identical to the left-hand side coefficient matrix of equations (3B.12), with the exception that θ and θ^* replace β and β^*, respectively. If it is assumed that $\beta = \beta^* = 0$, then the effect of a devaluation on the trade balance is, in the aggregate expenditure function version of the model, given by

$$
(3B.16) \qquad \frac{dB}{de} = \frac{1}{\Delta_{3B}} \{ m(L_i^* h^* - \bar{A}_i^* L_{\bar{Y}}^*)
$$
$$
+ m^*(L_i h - \bar{A}_i L_{\bar{Y}}) \, \Gamma^* \},
$$

where $\Gamma = \bar{A}_i f + F_i h$ and $\Gamma^* = \bar{A}_i^* f^* + X_i h^*$. Since $\Delta_{3B} > 0$, it follows that $dB/de \gtreqless 0$ as[2]

$$
(3B.17) \qquad |mL_i^* h\Gamma + mL_i h\Gamma^*| \gtreqless |m\bar{A}_i^* L_{\bar{Y}}^* \Gamma + m^* \bar{A}_i L_{\bar{Y}} \Gamma^*|.
$$

Although this is getting ahead of the story, it is interesting to note that one result that emerges from equation (3B.15) is that, in a two-country macroeconomic system, it is no longer

---

[2] Observe that the Marshall-Lerner condition plays no role here because it has been assumed that $\theta = \theta^* = 0$; i.e. that all supply curves are infinitely elastic. If this assumption is relaxed, then the Marshall-Lerner condition will have a role to play. See footnote 25 in Chapter 3.

true that equiproportional changes in the exchange rate, and home and foreign money supplies have the same impact (in absolute value terms) on the balance of trade. This follows from the fact that, in the absence of capital flows, interest rates are allowed to diverge in the two countries. Thus, exchange rate changes, which have a direct impact on the real value of the money supply in both countries, also have a direct impact on interest rates. Money supply changes, on the other hand, only affect interest rates *directly* in one country. (See Chapters 4 and 5 for a fuller discussion of this point.)

CHAPTER 4

Long-Run Adjustment
and the Role of Monetary and
Fiscal Policies

THUS FAR, the model developed in Chapter 3 has been used to examine the effect of exchange rate changes on the level of employment and output, as well as on the balance of trade, in Keynesian and Classical worlds. In this chapter, the basic model is extended in order to examine two topics of further interest. In section I the assumption of complete sterilization employed in Chapter 3 is relaxed, and the results of that chapter reexamined. In this analysis it is shown that, without complete sterilization, devaluations must be examined in terms of at least two sets of effects: short-run, or impact effects, and longer-term effects. This, in turn, permits a direct comparison of the results obtained here with those of the "monetarist" approach to payments analysis. In section III the roles of fiscal and monetary policy are examined. In addition to their intrinsic interest, the results obtained in this section provide a bridge to the Walrasian-type analysis of Chapter 5. Prior to this, however, section II digresses briefly in order to provide a diagramatic presentation of the complete model.

I THE MODEL WITHOUT COMPLETE STERILIZATION

A majority of relative price and/or income adjustment models of the balance of payments have included (explicitly or implicitly) an assumption of complete sterilization of the payments surplus or deficit by the monetary authorities. There are, however, at least two good reasons for considering an alternative specification of no, or at least less than perfect, sterilization. These are: (1) the assumption of complete sterilization imputes to the monetary authorities a greater degree of sophistication and control than they in fact possess, at least in the short run; and (2) as was just noted, relaxation of the sterilization assumption permits a comparison of the results obtained in an integrated elasticities-income framework with those derived in the "monetarist" framework. This comparison is especially interesting because it reveals that many of the monetarist results appear as special cases in the integrated model.

The Modified Model

Revision of the model developed in Chapter 3 in order to relax the assumption of complete sterilization turns out to be a more intricate exercise than might first appear, which may explain why it was attempted so infrequently prior to the rise of the monetarist approach. When attempted, the standard income approach was to specify an additional equation on the demand side of the model relating the nominal money supply, m, to the balance of payments. This equation usually took the form[1]

$$(4.1) \qquad m = m^a + \sigma B,$$

where m^a is the amount of nominal money supplied by the monetary authorities independent of balance of payments considerations (called here the autonomous money supply), and σ is the sterilization coefficient, assumed to be a constant. It is assumed that $0 \leq \sigma \leq 1$, where $\sigma = 0$ implies complete sterilization, while $\sigma = 1$ implies no sterilization. (As before, B is the net balance of trade.)

---

[1] See, for example, Takayama (1969).

Unfortunately, although popular in some places in the literature, in general this specification is not correct. As Aghevli and Borts (1973), Mundell (1968), and others have pointed out, careful consideration of equation (4.1) reveals that both m and m^a are stocks, while B is a flow. Unless $\sigma = 0$ or $B = 0$, equation (4.1) thus represents an invalid addition of a stock and a flow. In the general case, therefore, some other specification is required. One correct specification would be to rewrite equation (4.1) as

(4.1a) $m = m^a + R,$

where R is the stock of foreign exchange reserves. In this case total differentiation of equation (4.1a) yields

(4.2) $dm = dm^a + dR.$

But, since $dR = \sigma B$, this is equivalent to

(4.2a) $dm = dm^a + \sigma B.$

From equation (4.2a), it is clear that a general treatment of the nonsterilization case requires the addition of a time dimension to the model, and thus the construction of a complete dynamic system.

Such a dynamic model is beyond the scope of this study. However, although the general case can be treated only in a fully dynamic context, it is still possible to analyze the impact of incomplete sterilization in a comparative static framework by distinguishing between short- and long-run responses while considering only the case of initially balanced trade. In the short run, and starting from a point of initially balanced trade, the effects of a devaluation will be those developed in Chapter 3. This follows from the fact that the short run is defined to be a period of time too short for the surplus or deficit induced by a change in a control variable to have an effect on the system.

111

In the long run, without complete sterilization, it is obvious that, unless $B = 0$, the total money supply will be continuously changing. Thus, in the long run the money supply in fact becomes an endogenous variable in the system, and $B = 0$ must be imposed as an equilibrium condition.

With $B = 0$ imposed as an equilibrium condition, the most interesting question is the long-run effect of a devaluation on the level of output, and hence employment. However, before it can be assumed that the long-run equilibrium condition $B = 0$ in fact will be met, it is necessary to insure that changes in the money supply are in fact stabilizing. Since a deficit in the balance of trade implies that the money supply is falling, while a surplus implies the converse, it is necessary for stability that an increase in the money supply reduce a trade surplus and that a decrease in the money supply reduce a deficit—i.e. that $dB/dm < 0$. Unfortunately, as will be shown below, $dB/dm < 0$, which has been assumed to be true in the monetarist literature, need not hold in either the Keynesian or Classical versions of the model. However, if both goods are gross substitutes, an overly strong sufficient condition to guarantee $dB/dm < 0$ in both systems is that the Marshall-Lerner condition be met.

Long-Run Adjustment: The Keynesian System

To establish the response of the trade balance to a change in the nominal stock of money, the Keynesian model developed in Chapter 3 must be solved for dB/dm. In the general version of the model this yields

$$(4.3) \qquad \frac{dB}{dm} = -\frac{1}{\Delta_3} \left\{ \frac{F_i}{L_i} [1 - D_y + \beta(D_{eq} - X_{p/e})] \right.$$
$$\left. + \frac{D_i}{L_i} [F_y - \beta X(1 + \eta_X + \eta_F)] \right\},$$

while the aggregate expenditure function version yields

$$(4.3a) \qquad \frac{dB}{dm} = -\frac{1}{\Delta_4}\left\{\frac{F_i}{L_i} h(1 + \beta X)\right.$$
$$\left. + \frac{\bar{A}_i}{L_i}[f - \beta X(1 + \eta_X + \eta_F)]\right\}.$$

A comparison of equations (4.3) and (4.3a) with (3.33) and (3.34) quickly reveals that $dB/de > 0$ and $dB/dm > 0$ are not incompatible events. Thus, the assumption that a devaluation improves the trade balance does not insure that changes in the money supply will be stabilizing. However, as equations (4.3) and (4.3a) indicate, the combination of gross substitutability and the meeting of the Marshall-Lerner condition insures that $dB/dm < 0$, and, therefore, that the system is stable in the long run.[2] Moreover, as long as the trade balance is negatively related to changes in the stock of money, it does not matter whether a devaluation improves the balance of trade or causes it to deteriorate. In either event the economy will be stable, and trade-related changes in the money supply eventually will bring the trade account back into balance. Thus, as long as the system is stable in the long run, with $dB/dm < 0$, a Keynesian

---

[2] It can be noted in passing that, if the aggregate supply curve is infinitely elastic ($\beta = 0$), then stability is insured, while if goods demand is not responsive to the interest rate (i.e. if $F_i = D_i = 0$), then $dB/dm = 0$, and it would be necessary to incorporate a real-balance effect before monetary changes would affect the trade balance.

It is also interesting to note that, in the case of equation (4.3a), the added structure imposed by the aggregate expenditure function implies that, with a positively sloped supply curve, the Marshall-Lerner condition alone is sufficient to insure long-run stability.

Finally, it can be observed that this result contrasts with similar analyses in the monetarist framework, where $dB/de < 0$ always. Of course, the framework in which the various monetarist studies have been carried out is more like the Classical version of the model developed here, rather than the Keynesian. However, as will be shown below, this same problem—that $dB/dm < 0$ is not guaranteed—carries over to the Classical version of the model as well.

system will behave in essentially the same fashion as the price-specie-flow world of Hume, a fact first noted by Mundell (1961). However, it is worth repeating that this long-run stability is not insured.

The fact that stability is not insured is readily understandable if either equation (4.3) or (4.3a) is examined carefully. Note that, if $\beta = 0$, then $dB/dm < 0$ always. This says that, if the economy is in the "extreme Keynesian" range of the aggregate supply function, no price effects accompany an expansionary monetary policy. In this case, both the drop in interest rates and the expansion in output and income that accompanies an increase in the money supply lead to a rise in imports. With exports dependent only on prices and the exchange rate, neither of which has changed, the result must be a deterioration of the trade account. When $\beta > 0$, however, expansionary monetary policy also increases the price of the domestically produced good. In this case, without gross substitutability, and without the Marshall-Lerner condition's being met, price effects tend to offset the income effects. They still need not dominate, that is, even if $(1 + \eta_X + \eta_F) > 0$, and $(D_{eq} - X_{p/e}) < 0$ it would still be the case that $dB/dm < 0$ if

$$(4.4) \qquad \left| \frac{F_i}{L_i}(1 - D_y) + \frac{D_i}{L_i} F_y \right| > \left| \beta(D_{eq} - X_{p/e}) \frac{F_i}{L_i} \right.$$
$$\left. - \beta X(1 + \eta_X + \eta_F) \frac{D_i}{L_i} \right|,$$

but they may.

If it is assumed that both goods are gross substitutes and that the Marshall-Lerner condition is met, so that long-run stability is guaranteed, the longer-term effects of a devaluation are readily established. Without sterilization, the money supply becomes an endogenous variable, dependent on the short-run balance of trade. Specifically, if a devaluation alters the trade balance, so that $B \neq 0$, then the cumulative change in the stock of money as a result of the devaluation will be given by $\rho = \int_0^T B(t)\, dt$, where T is the time at which $B = 0$ again. Since the departure of the trade balance from zero is the result of a change in the exchange rate, in a long-run comparative-static model, it is sufficient to include in the model the equation

$$(4.5) \qquad \frac{dm}{de} = \rho,$$

with, of course, the sign of (4.5) the same as the sign of dB/de.

Since balanced trade is insured in the long run as long as $dB/dm < 0$, and as long as the monetary authorities do not run out of foreign exchange reserves before a new equilibrium is reached if $B < 0$, all that remains is to determine the long-run effect of a devaluation on the level of output and employment. Solving for dY/de in this long-run framework and assuming that $dB/de > 0$ yields

$$(4.6) \qquad \frac{dY}{de} = \frac{1}{\Delta_3}\left\{ D_{eq} - X_{p/e} + \frac{D_i}{L_i}\left[\rho - (1 - \alpha)(1 - \mu)m\right]\right\}$$

or, with an aggregate expenditure function

$$(4.6a) \qquad \frac{dY}{de} = -\frac{1}{\Delta_4}\left\{ X(1 + \eta_X + \eta_F - h) \right.$$
$$\left. - \frac{\bar{A}_i - F_i}{L_i}\left[\rho - (1 - \alpha)(1 - \mu)m\right]\right\}.$$

Given the assumptions made thus far, it is clear that the sign of dY/de depends on the magnitude of μ. If $\mu \geq 1$, then $dY/de > 0$. If $\mu < 1$, but $\rho > (1 - \alpha)(1 - \mu)m$, then $dY/de > 0$ again. If $\mu < 1$ and $\rho < (1 - \alpha)(1 - \mu)m$, then $dY/de > 0$ if

$$(4.7) \qquad |D_{eq} - X_{p/e}| > \left| \frac{D_i}{L_i}\left[\rho - (1 - \alpha)(1 - \mu)m\right]\right|,$$

or, equivalently, in the aggregate expenditure function case, if

$$(4.7a) \qquad \left| X(1 + \eta_X + \eta_F - h) \right| \\ > \left| \frac{\bar{A}_i - F_i}{L_i} [\rho - (1 - \alpha)(1 - \mu)m] \right|.$$

Intuitively, the various possibilities implied by equation (4.6) are readily explained. Given the assumptions made above, a devaluation will lead to a short-run improvement in the trade balance. If it has also led to a short-run increase in the level of employment and output (i.e. if $D_{eq} - X_{p/e} - (D_i/L_i)(1 - \alpha)(1 - \mu)m > 0$), then it also will lead to a long-run improvement. That is, the effect of the increase in the money supply resulting from the trade surplus will be to increase further output and employment until, with a positive marginal propensity to import, income has risen enough to generate an increase in the value of imports sufficient to match the increased value of exports. If the devaluation led to a decrease in output and employment in the short run, then this may prevail in the long run as well if the income elasticity of demand for real cash balances is low enough and the interest elasticity of demand for goods high enough. In this case, the increase in the nominal money supply resulting from the trade surplus will reduce the interest rate and increase the demand for domestic and foreign goods. If import demand is sufficiently interest-elastic, this may result in trade once again being balanced *before* output and employment have regained their old levels. In this case, the long-run expansionary monetary effects of the devaluation will succeed only in mitigating, but not reversing, the negative short-run effects. Of course, this need not happen. Depending on the values of the various parameters in the system, it may be the case that, even if the devaluation reduces output and employment in the short run, it will raise them in the longer term.

116

In general, it is not possible to pin down the sign of dY/de in the long run more than this. However, since the change in the money supply must be sufficient to reverse any exchange rate effects on the balance of payments, thus insuring that $B = 0$ in the long run, an examination of dB/de and dB/dm suggests that $\rho \simeq m$ may be necessary to restore equilibrium,[3] which in turn implies that $dY/de > 0$ is the usual case.

It is interesting to note that, in this case, if the monetary authorities follow a Keynesian neutral monetary policy of pegging the interest rate, this will have the dual effect of achieving the equivalent of a conscious policy of sterilization while eliminating the possibility of negative employment effects accompanying a devaluation. Note also that, in one sense, Keynesian neutral monetary policy is "destabilizing," although not in the sense of Tsiang. With the monetary authorities attempting to peg the interest rate, even if the Marshall-Lerner condition is satisfied and all goods are gross substitutes, a long-run equilibrium with $B = 0$ will not be attained. However, it is obvious that this is not instability in the same sense that either $dB/dm > 0$ or an IS curve with a greater slope than an LM curve in a model with the Samuelson adjustment mechanism implies instability.

Long-Run Adjustment: The Classical System

As was true in the Keynesian system, the Classical system also requires $dB/dm < 0$ to insure long-run stability. In the Classical version of the model, however, if $dB/de > 0$, then $dB/dm < 0$, and conversely. Thus, as long as a devaluation improves the trade balance in the short run, the economy will be stable in the long run. Since gross substitutability and the Marshall-Lerner condition's being met, together constitute an overly

---

[3] As will be shown below, in the Classical case $\rho \equiv m$ always.

strong sufficient condition to insure that $dB/de > 0$, this obviously will also suffice to insure that $dB/dm < 0$.

Solving the Classical version of the model for dB/dm yields

$$(4.8) \qquad \frac{dB}{dm} = -\frac{1}{\Delta_5} \left\{ \frac{F_i}{L_i} [1 - D_y + \theta(D_{eq} - X_{p/e})] \right.$$
$$\left. + \frac{D_i}{L_i} [F_y - \theta X(1 + \eta_X + \eta_F)] \right\},$$

which is identical to equation (4.3) except that θ appears in place of β. A comparison of equation (4.8) with equation (3.47), which is reproduced here as equation (4.9) for convenience,

$$(4.9) \qquad \frac{dB}{de} = \frac{m}{\Delta_5} \left\{ \frac{F_i}{L_i} [1 - D_y + \theta(D_{eq} - X_{p/e})] \right.$$
$$\left. + \frac{D_i}{L_i} [F_y - \theta X(1 + \eta_X + \eta_F)] \right\},$$

reveals that $dB/dm = -(1/m)(dB/de)$, or, since units were chosen initially so that $e \equiv 1$, that $dB/(dm/m) = -dB/(de/e)$. Thus, in absolute magnitude, equiproportional changes in the money supply and the exchange rate can be seen to have equal impacts on the balance of trade. Moreover, the sign of dB/dm is, clearly, the negative of the sign of dB/de. Thus, a result that has been reported in the macroeconomic monetarist literature, and by Kemp (1970) and Krueger (1974) in more Walrasian settings, is seen to hold in an integrated elasticities/absorption framework as well. However, as is clear from equation (4.8), there is no guarantee that $dB/dm < 0$. In the model developed here, with its complete goods market, the sign of dB/dm (and, of course dB/de) depends on the relative magnitude of various parameters in the system. This is in sharp contrast with the monetarist literature where $dB/de > 0$ always,[4] and stability

[4] See, for example, Dornbush (1973b), Frenkel and Rodriquez (1975), Johnson (1972), and Mundell (1968). In the Walrasian analysis of Dornbush,

is insured. Moreover, contrary to the monetarist literature, where the Marshall-Lerner condition plays no role in the analysis, it is seen here to be an integral part of the model. In fact, if an aggregate expenditure function is employed (as in most of macroeconomic monetarist studies) the expression for dB/dm is simply

$$(4.10) \qquad \frac{dB}{dm} = -\frac{1}{\Delta_6}\left\{\frac{F_i}{L_i}h(1 + \beta X) \right.$$

$$\left. + \frac{\overline{A}_i}{L_i}[f - \beta X(1 + \eta_X + \eta_F)]\right\},$$

and the Marshall-Lerner condition alone is sufficient to insure stability.

If it is assumed that $dB/dm < 0$, then it is readily established that, in the long run, $dY/de = 0$. Making use of equation (4.5), and requiring that $B = 0$, then yields (in the general case)

$$(4.11) \qquad \frac{dY}{de} = \frac{1}{\Delta_5}\frac{D_i}{L_i}(\rho - m).$$

However, since $dB/(de/e) = -dB(dm/m)$, to obtain balance in the trade account after a devaluation requires that $dm/m = de/e$, or, equivalently, that $dm/de = m/e$. However, since units were chosen initially so that $e \equiv 1$, this is equivalent to $dm/de = m$. However, from equation (4.5), it is clear that this means that $\rho = m$, so that, in the Classical system $dY/de = 0$.

---

the analysis applies only to the trade balance, since there are no capital flows in the model, and the result is obtained that the balance of payments unambiguously improves with a devaluation. In the more macroeconomic model of Frenkel and Rodriguez, the balance of payments is divided into trade, debt service, monetary, and capital accounts. Here, it is found that, in the short run, the trade and capital accounts improve, while the debt service account deteriorates and the overall balance of payments improves. Similar results can be found in the work of Johnson and Mundell, as well as in other places in the monetarist literature.

Intuitively, of course, this is readily explained, and follows directly from the homogeneity properties of the Classical system. With an assumption of homogeneity, a change in a money price will, if the money supply is an endogenous variable, lead to a change in all other prices and the money supply in the same proportion. But, as was noted above, when there is less than perfect sterilization, the domestic money supply has in fact become an endogenous variable in the long run. Thus the long-run effect of a change in the exchange rate (which is, of course, simply another money price) will be an equiproportional change in the money supply, with no change in any real variable.

Long-Run Adjustment: A Final Comment

In both the Keynesian and Classical systems, the fact that an adjustment mechanism much like Hume's operates to restore external balance so long as the monetary authorities do not sterilize the payments surplus or deficit (and, of course, so long as an increase in the money supply causes the trade balance to deteriorate and vice versa) has clear policy significance. It suggests that countries need to take positive action to correct a payments surplus or deficit either because the adjustment process takes too long (in the sense that foreign exchange reserves would be exhausted before equilibrium is restored), or, in a Keynesian world, because an (assumed to be) expansionary devaluation is more appealing to the government than a contractionary adjustment via a reduction in the money supply. In the Classical system, of course, only the former reason remains as a rational explanation for direct policy action.

II THE COMPLETE MODEL: A DIAGRAMMATIC DIGRESSION

In light of the complexities of the model in both the short and long run, it seems useful to digress somewhat at this point and present some of the principal results diagrammatically, employing the aggregate demand, aggregate supply, and balance of payments equilibrium curves developed in Chapter 3. Unfortunately, as the formal analysis has indicated, in both the Keynesian and Classical systems there are few results which are determinate on *a priori* theoretical grounds. Rather than present a complete taxonomy of all possible cases, it will be assumed that the simple Marshall-Lerner condition is met and that both goods in the model are gross substitutes. Furthermore, it will be assumed that income and/or price effects dominate interest rate effects, so that the balance of payments equilibrium line has a negative slope (i.e. multiple equilibria are ruled out). Finally, in the Keynesian case, it will be assumed that a devaluation unambiguously improves the balance of trade, and raises the level of output and employment.

The Keynesian System

Given the preceding assumptions, the model can be represented graphically as in Figure 4.1.[5] Figure 4.1 reflects an initial condition of balanced trade. If the economy is in the region above the balance of payments equilibrium line, there is a deficit, while a surplus prevails if it is in the region below it. (In all cases, it is of course true that the actual values for prices and output are given by the intersection of the aggregate demand (DD) and aggregate supply (SS) curves.)

To use Figure 4.1 to analyze the effects of exchange rate changes requires knowledge of how the various curves shift when control variables change. Since in the Keynesian system it is obvious that $dY^s/de = dY^s/dm = 0$, to portray impact effects requires that the signs of dY^d/de and dY^B/de be known. In addition, since $dm \neq 0$ whenever $B \neq 0$, to indicate

---

[5] Note that, in light of the assumptions made, the aggregate demand curve has a greater slope (in absolute value) than does the balance of payments equilibrium line.

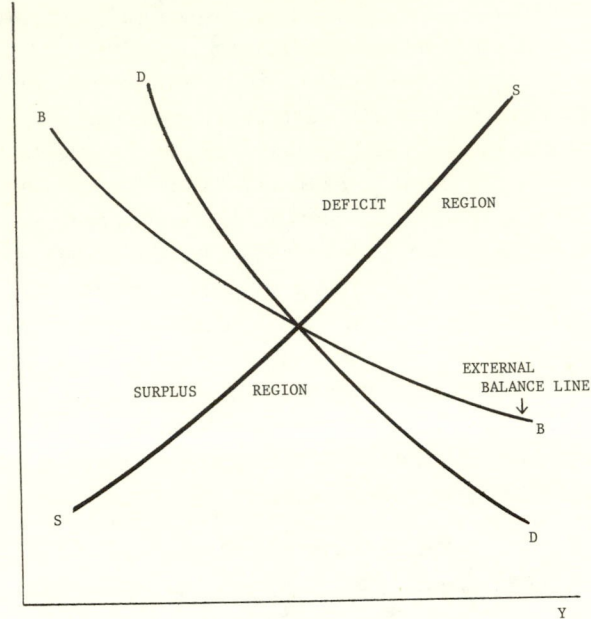

Figure 4.1

long-run effects requires knowledge of the signs of dY^d/dm and dY^B/dm. For the general specification of the model, these expressions can be shown to be[6]

$$(4.12) \quad \frac{dY^d}{de} = \frac{1}{\Delta_1}\left[D_{eq} - X_{p/e} - \frac{D_i}{L_i}m(1 - \alpha)(1 - \mu)\right],$$

$$(4.13) \quad \frac{dY^B}{de} = -\frac{1}{\Delta_2}\left[X(1 + \eta_X + \eta_F) - \frac{F_i}{L_i}m(1 - \alpha)(1 - \mu)\right],$$

$$(4.14) \quad \frac{dY^d}{dm} = \frac{1}{\Delta_1}\frac{D_i}{L_i},$$

[6] See the equation for dY^d and dY^B in Appendix A to the previous chapter.

122

and

$$(4.15) \qquad \frac{dY^B}{dm} = - \frac{1}{\Delta_2} \frac{F_i}{L_i},$$

where $\Delta_1 = 1 - D_y + (D_i/L_i)L_{\bar{Y}}$ and $\Delta_2 = F_y - (F_i/L_i)L_{\bar{Y}}$. For the absorption function case, the equivalent results are

$$(4.16) \qquad \frac{dY^d}{de} = - \frac{1}{\Delta_{1a}} \left[X(1 + \eta_X + \eta_F - h) \right.$$
$$\left. + \frac{\bar{A}_i - F_i}{L_i} m(1 - \alpha)(1 - \mu) \right],$$

$$(4.17) \qquad \frac{dY^d}{dm} = \frac{1}{\Delta_{1a}} \frac{\bar{A}_i - F_i}{L_i},$$

where $\Delta_{1a} = h + f + [(\bar{A}_i - F_i)/L_i]L_{\bar{Y}}$. Equations (4.14) and (4.16) turn out to be the expressions for dY^B/de and dY^B/dm for this case as well as for the general specification.

Given all assumptions made thus far, dY^d/de, dY^d/dm and $dY^B/de > 0$, while $dY^B/dm < 0$,[7] and a devaluation unambiguously increases the level of output (and employment) and generates a surplus in the balance of trade in the short run. Thus, the impact effects of a devaluation can be graphed as in Figure 4.2, where now primed curves represent short-run positions after the devaluation. The trade surplus is reflected in the fact that now the balance of payments equilibrium line lies above the aggregate demand curve at the equilibrium level of output.

Since now $B > 0$, $dm/dt > 0$, and the domestic nominal money supply is growing. From equations (4.15) and (4.16) it is clear that this will cause the aggregate demand curve to shift to the right and the trade balance equilibrium curve to shift to the left. This process will continue until $B = 0$ again,

---

[7] Since relative price and/or income effects are assumed to dominate interest rate effects, even if $\mu > 1$, $dY^B/de > 0$.

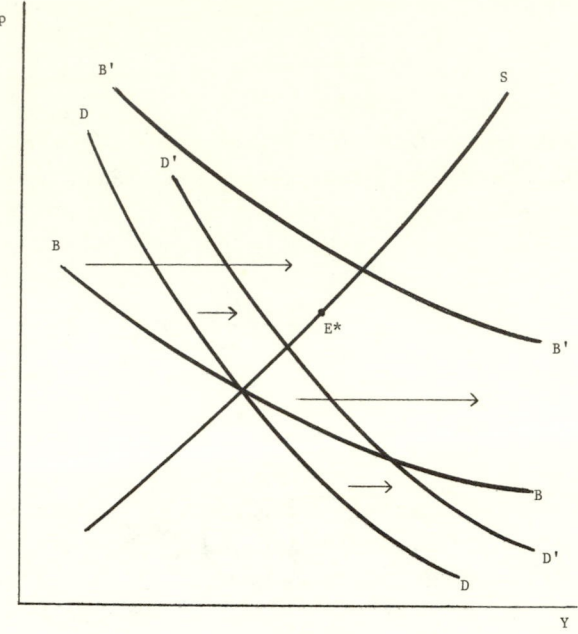

Figure 4.2

and the entire economy is in equilibrium. Obviously this will take place only when the aggregate supply, aggregate demand, and balance of payments equilibrium curves all intersect at the same point. Equally obvious is the fact that, in this case, this will be at a higher level of output (and prices) than before. (Long-run equilibrium will be at a point such as point E* in Figure 4.2.)

Perhaps a better way to see what is going on is to note that there are, in effect, two $B = 0$ curves, a long-run one and a short-run one. To construct the long-run curve, it is only necessary to realize that, given the exchange rate, there are separate short-run demand and balance of payments curves for each possible stock of nominal money and, given the assumptions made here, one point where they intersect. If,

124

as in Figure 4.3, a line is drawn connecting the point on each of the short-run demand curves where trade is balanced, a locus is obtained that may be thought of as the long-run external balance line. Since in the case portrayed here, any devaluation shifts both the short-run demand and balance of payments curves to the right, the long-run external balance line will also shift to the right with a devaluation.

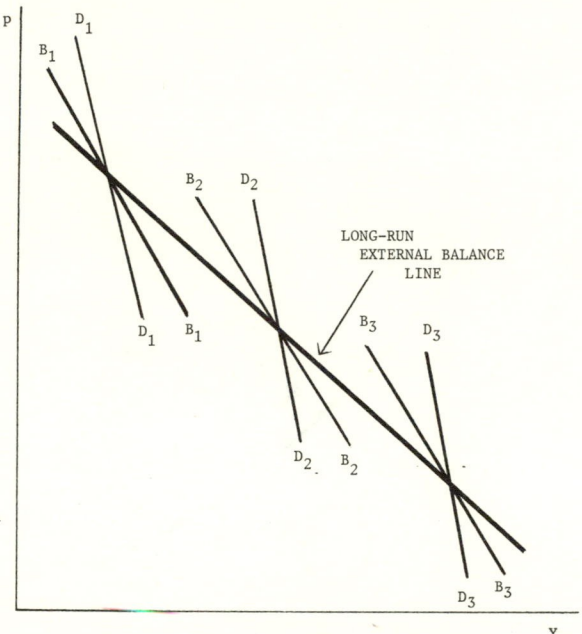

Figure 4.3

One of the assumptions made in constructing the model was that aggregate demand equals aggregate supply. Therefore, to be in equilibrium the economy must be on both the external balance (EE) and aggregate supply (SS) curves.[8] Anywhere

[8] The aggregate supply curve is not exactly the same as a Mundellian internal balance line, since along it employment is changing.

else, adjustments are taking place that will move the economy toward the intersection of these two curves. Thus, ultimately, the long-run model can be represented graphically by two curves, as in Figure 4.4. A devaluation shifts the EE curve to the right, to E'E', and leads to a new long-run equilibrium at point A', where trade is balanced, the money supply is higher, and both output and employment have increased.

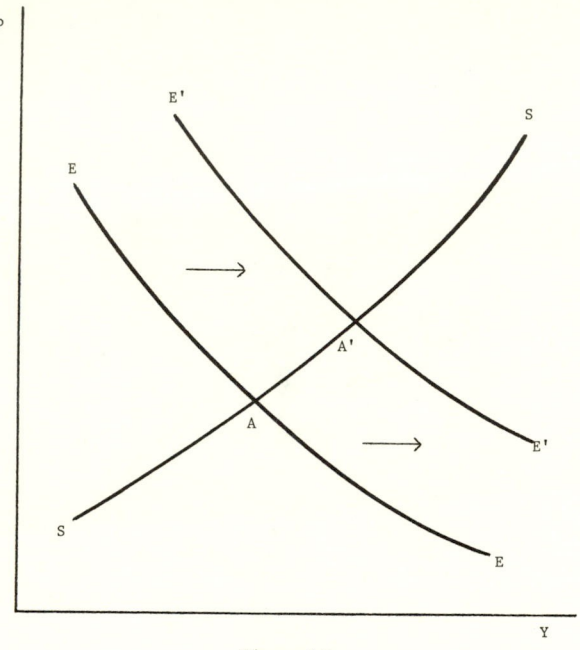

Figure 4.4

Although not all cases will be examined here, the workings of the model are perhaps easier to see if some cases of potential long-run instability also are examined. Note that, in Figure 4.3, the aggregate demand and short-run external balance lines associated with each possible stock of nominal money were drawn under the assumption that, at ever larger stocks of money and with a fixed exchange rate, the two curves intersected at a lower domestic price and higher output. That is, they were drawn under the assumption that the long-run external balance line had a negative slope. However, as an examination of the underlying equations will reveal, it is possible for the long-run external balance line to be positively sloped even if the underlying short-run curves have negative slopes. If the long-run external balance line has a slope that is positive but less than the slope of the aggregate supply curve, then the model will still be stable. If the slope of the aggregate supply curve is less than that of the external balance line, long-run instability will result.

This may be illustrated with the aid of Figures 4.5 and 4.6. In Figure 4.5, the slope of the external balance line is less than that of the aggregate supply curve. If the economy is initially

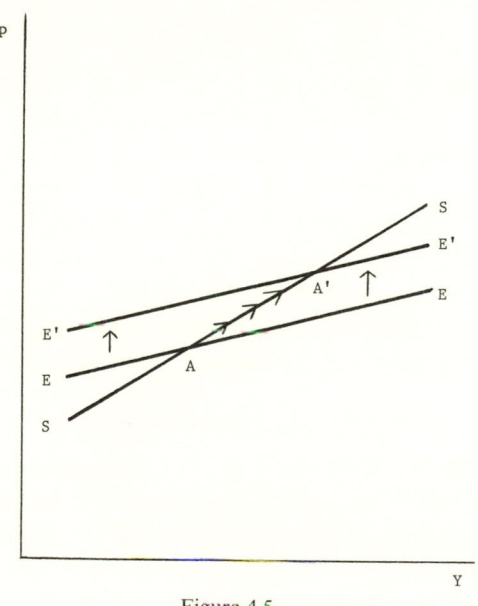

Figure 4.5

127

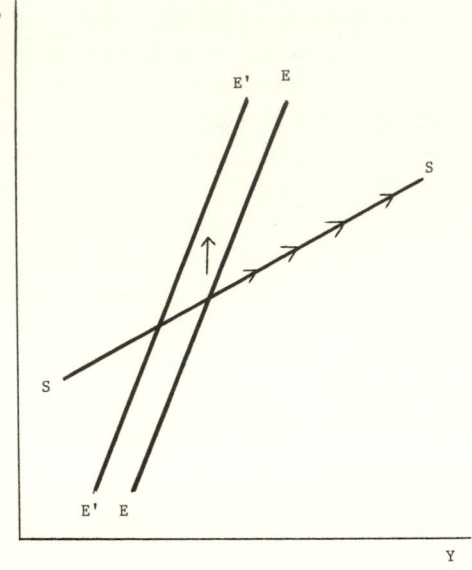

Figure 4.6

in equilibrium at point A, a devaluation that improves the trade balance in the short run will, in this case, shift the long-run external balance line upward from EE to E'E'. In this case the adjustment process, as the money supply rises with the surplus, will carry the economy to a new equilibrium at point A', as indicated by the arrows. If, however, the slope of the external balance line exceeds that of the aggregate supply curve, as in Figure 4.6, then a devaluation will be destabilizing as the economy moves in the direction indicated by the arrows.

The Classical System

With the necessary infrastructure developed extensively in the preceding subsection, a diagrammatic representation of the Classical system can be presented fairly quickly. It was demonstrated in Chapter 3 that the only significant difference between the Classical and Keynesian systems is that, in the former, the aggregate supply curve also is shifted by changes in the exchange rate. This, together with the fact that even a successful devaluation unambiguously lowers the level of output and employment in the short run, implies that the impact effect of a devaluation in a Classical world can be illustrated as in Figure 4.7. In the short run, the devaluation shifts the aggregate supply curve from SS to S'S', while aggregate demand is shifted from DD to D'D', and the short-run external balance line from BB to B'B'. Since stability has been assumed, B'B' lies above D'D' at the new short-run equilibrium level of output, so that a surplus has developed.

In the longer term, the increase in the money supply shifts the aggregate demand curve to the right, while the external

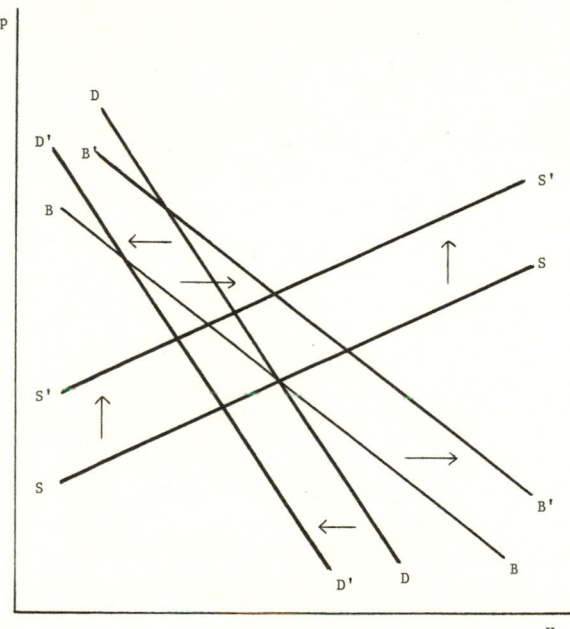

Figure 4.7

129

balance curve shifts to the left. Since, in the long run, a devaluation will not change output and employment in a Classical system, the long-run equilibrium will be at a higher price but the same output as before the change. In Figure 4.8 long-run equilibrium is portrayed, and a devaluation has the effect of inducing an equiproportional shift in the aggregate demand and long-run external balance curves. The price level is higher, but there is no change in any real variable.

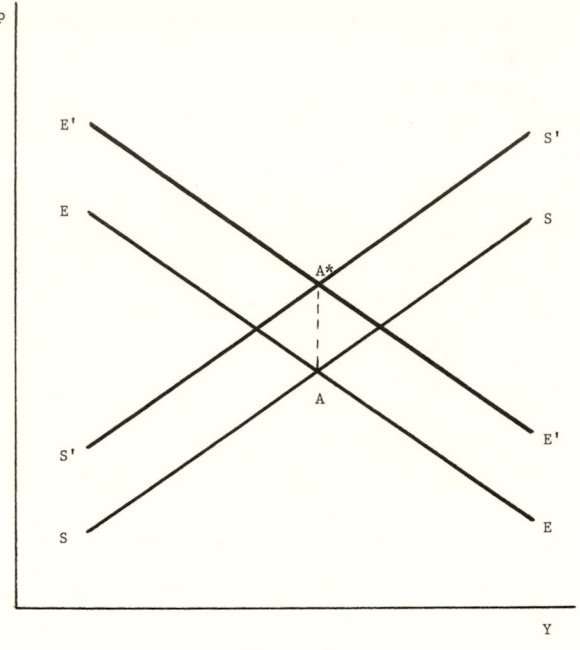

Figure 4.8

III MONETARY AND FISCAL POLICIES

In this section, the effectiveness of monetary and fiscal policies in the fixed-exchange-rate open economy described by the integrated model is examined in more detail. Of course, as the results of section I of this chapter indicate, without complete sterilization monetary policy is ineffective in the long run in both the Keynesian and the Classical systems (with the obvious proviso that the system be stable). However, additional insights into the workings of the model can be gained by examining the short-run effects of changes in the nominal money supply (or, what is the same thing, by examining monetary policy under the assumption of complete sterilization) under both Keynesian and Classical conditions. Thus, the first part of this section is devoted to such an examination. Then, to round out the picture, fiscal policy is examined in terms of both short-run and long-run effects. Here, the interesting result emerges that the nature of the government's expenditure pattern, together with two key elasticities may, in some cases, determine whether or not fiscal policy is effective.

Monetary Policy under Complete Sterilization

In a reexamination of the relationship between changes in the nominal money supply and the balance of trade in a Walrasian setting, Kemp (1970) presented a proof that equiproportional devaluations of the domestic currency and reductions in the nominal money supply have identical effects on the trade balance. This result, which was one of the principal conclusions of the paper and which represented a generalization of a result first obtained by Hahn (1959), subsequently was reported in various articles in the monetarist literature (e.g. Dornbush (1973b), Frenkel and Rodriguez (1975). As was demonstrated in section I of this chapter, this result also holds in the Classical version of the model developed in Chapter 3. However, as was also demonstrated in section I, in a Keynesian system, equiproportional changes in the nominal money supply and the exchange rate have quite different (short-run/sterilized) effects on the balance of trade. As with many other properties of the Keynesian model, this stems from the assumption of a fixed

131

money wage and the resulting infinitely elastic supply curve for labor. The fixed money wage rate assumption implies that the aggregate supply curve is independent of the exchange rate, which means that a devaluation only shifts the aggregate demand curve. For the Classical system, however, the specification of the labor market requires that the exchange rate appear as one of the arguments of the labor supply function. This results in the aggregate supply curve's shifting with a devaluation, which offsets many of the effects of the shift of the aggregate demand curve.

A particularly illuminating way to compare the workings of the two versions of the model is to reexamine this result. To do this, it is useful to look at the equation giving aggregate demand for the domestic good *without* integrating the financial market into it. This can be done by taking equations (3.1) through (3.4), (3.6), and (3.8), totally differentiating, then solving for dY^d. This gives

$$(4.18) \qquad dY^d = \frac{1}{1 - D_y} [(D_{eq} - X_{p/e}) \, de$$
$$- (D_{eq} - X_{p/e}) \, dp + D_i \, di].$$

For the aggregate expenditure function this becomes

$$(4.19) \qquad dY^d = \frac{1}{h + f} [X(1 + \eta_X + \eta_F - h)$$
$$\times (dp - de) + (\bar{A}_i - F_i) \, di].$$

From Chapter 3, it will be recalled that the demand side of the model is identical in both the Keynesian and Classical systems, while the supply sides differ. For the Keynesian case, the total differential of the aggregate supply function is

$$(4.20) \qquad dY^s = \frac{1}{\beta} dp,$$

while for the Classical case it is

$$(4.21) \qquad dY^s = \frac{1}{\theta}[dp - de].$$

To take the Classical case first, if equation (4.21) is used to solve for dp, this expression substituted into equations (4.18) or (4.19) and use made of the fact that, in equilibrium, $dY^d = dY^s = dY$, then

$$(4.22) \qquad dY = \left[\frac{D_i}{1 - D_y + \theta(D_{eq} - X_{p/e})}\right] di,$$

or

$$(4.23) \qquad dY = \left[\frac{\bar{A}_i - F_i}{h + f - \theta X(1 + \eta_X + \eta_F - h)}\right] di.$$

From either equation (4.22) or (4.23) it is apparent that changes in the exchange rate have no *direct* effect on equilibrium output since any exchange-rate induced changes in demand are exactly offset by changes in supply. Of course, the effect of changes in the interest rate still appears. When the complete system is solved, it becomes clear that a devaluation affects equilibrium output by affecting the interest rate. But this, of course, is exactly the way in which changes in the supply of nominal money affect the system. The result is that both the exchange rate and the money supply affect the balance of payments in the same fashion, and, therefore, equiproportional changes in them have the same impact on the trade balance. That this is not true for the Keynesian system follows by solving for dp from equation (4.20) and using this in either equation (4.18) or (4.19) to find dY. This yields

$$(4.24) \qquad dY = \frac{1}{\Delta_7}[(D_{eq} - X_{p/e})\,de + D_i\,di],$$

or

$$(4.25) \qquad dY = \frac{1}{\Delta_8}\left[D_i\, di - X(1 + \eta_X + \eta_F - h)\, de\right],$$

where $\Delta_7 = 1 - D_y + \beta(D_{eq} - X_{p/e})$, and $\Delta_8 = h + f - \beta X(1 + \eta_X + \eta_F - h)$. From either of these equations it is clear that there is both a direct effect of the devaluation and, when the financial market is included, an indirect effect via induced changes in the interest rate.

An interesting implication of the fact that, in the Classical system, $dB/(de/e) = dB/(dm/m)$ is that, with complete sterilization in an open economy, money is not neutral, even in a Classical world. A favorite textbook exercise is to demonstrate that even in the short run, in closed-economy Classical models money is merely a "veil." That is, a change in the supply of nominal money does nothing to alter "real" variables in the system, but, instead, affects only the price level. However in an open economy in the short run, or in the long run also, if the monetary authorities follow a policy of complete sterilization, this is clearly not true. The symmetry in effects between $dB/(de/e)$ and $dB/(dm/m)$ is matched by a symmetry between $dY/(de/e)$ and $dY/(dm/m)$. Thus, solving for $dY/(dm/m)$ yields

$$(4.26) \qquad \frac{dY}{dm/m} = \frac{m}{\Delta_5}\frac{D_i}{L_i}$$

or, with an aggregate expenditure function,

$$(4.27) \qquad \frac{dY}{dm/m} = \frac{m}{\Delta_6}\frac{\bar{A}_i - F_i}{L_i}.$$

Equation (4.26) is the negative of equation (3.45), while equation (4.27) is the negative of equation (3.46). This result follows from the assumption of complete sterilization and the fact that, in an open economy, the aggregate supply function is not a vertical line. Even with flexible money wage rates and prices, an increase in the money supply results in wages increasing by only a fraction of the price increase (specifically, $dw = \alpha\, dp$). This is equivalent to a rightward shift of the labor supply function as graphed in the $(w/p, N)$ plane, and, given a downward sloping demand function, an increase in employment and output. It is not unless the complete sterilization assumption is dropped that $dY/de = dY/dm = 0$.

Fiscal Policy in the Short and Long Run

As was noted above, in the long run, without complete sterilization, monetary policy is obviously completely ineffective in both Keynesian and Classical worlds (as long as these worlds are stable.)[9] In the short run, it should be readily apparent that an expansionary fiscal policy will, if gross substitutability and the Marshall-Lerner condition both are met, have the usual results of expanding output and generating a deficit in the trade balance. However, more interesting results emerge when the effect of fiscal policy is examined in a long-run nonsterilization framework. In this case, it turns out to be necessary to distinguish between general expansionary fiscal policy and a "buy domestic" policy.

The general specification of the demand side of the model means that it is possible to distinguish between an increase in demand that applies only to domestically produced goods (a "buy domestic" policy) and one that is simply a general increase in expenditure (i.e. government spending increases on both domestic and foreign goods). To do this it is only necessary to rewrite equations (3.4) and (3.5) as

$$(4.28) \qquad D = D(y, p, eq, i) + \gamma$$

---

[9] One useful way to regard monetary policy may be to recall that, as derived in section III, neither the long-run external balance line nor the supply curve are shifted by any changes in the nominal money supply. Thus, since their intersection determines the long-run equilibrium position of the economy, this too will not be changed.

and

(4.29) $\qquad F = F(y, p, eq, i) + \zeta$

where γ and ζ are shift parameters representing any exogenous change in the demand for the two goods. With these two equations, it is possible to consider three distinct cases of fiscal policy: (1) the government follows a "buy domestic" policy, so that $d\gamma > 0$ while $d\zeta = 0$; (2) the government follows a general policy of increased net expenditures without regard to source, so that $d\gamma > 0$ and $d\zeta > 0$; and (3) the government follows a (highly unlikely) "buy foreign" policy, so that $d\gamma = 0$ while $d\zeta > 0$.

For each of these three cases, it would appear to be possible to examine the results of such policies in either a Keynesian or Classical system. However, recall that the only difference between the two systems was on the aggregate supply side of the model. In a Keynesian world, aggregate supply was seen to depend only on the price of the domestic good, so that the total differential of the aggregate supply function was $dY^s = \hat{\beta}\, dp$ (where $\hat{\beta} = 1/\beta$). In a Classical world, where aggregate supply was seen to depend on domestic prices and the exchange rate, the total differential was $dY^s = \hat{\theta}\,(dp - de)$ ($\hat{\theta} = 1/\theta$). However, with both $\hat{\theta}$ and $\hat{\beta} > 0$, and with exchange rates fixed, so that $de = 0$, the only difference in the two cases will be the difference in magnitude between $\hat{\theta}$ and $\hat{\beta}$ (i.e. in the slopes of the two aggregate supply curves). Thus, any results valid in one context will, except for a scalar factor, also be valid in the other.

With this in mind, consider first the case where the government follows an explicit "buy domestic" policy. In the short run, it is easy to establish that[10]

(4.30) $\qquad \dfrac{dY}{d\gamma} = \dfrac{1}{\Delta_3}$

[10] See the appendix to this chapter.

136

while

(4.31) $\qquad \dfrac{dB}{d\gamma} = -\dfrac{1}{\Delta_3}\left\{ F_y - \dfrac{F_i}{L_i} L_{\bar{Y}} \right.$

$$-\beta \left[\dfrac{F_i}{L_i}(\alpha m + (1 - \alpha)yL_{\bar{Y}}) \right.$$

$$\left.\left. + X(1 + \eta_X + \eta_F) \right] \right\}.$$

Since $\Delta_3 > 0$, it is clear that the short-run effects of an expansionary fiscal policy will in fact be expansionary (i.e. $dY/d\gamma > 0$). To determine the sign of $dB/d\gamma$, it is necessary to determine the sign of the numerator. Note, first, that the terms $F_y - (F_i/L_i) L_{\bar{Y}}$ comprise the denominator of the equation determining the slope of the short-run external balance line, while the portion of the numerator in square brackets is the numerator of the same equation (see equation (3.18)). If it is assumed that income and/or price effects always dominate interest rate effects, so that both the numerator and denominator of equation (3.18) are positive, and, therefore, that the short-run external balance line has a negative slope,[11] then, with $\Delta_3 > 0$, $dB/d\gamma < 0$. Thus, in the "usual" case, fiscal policy expands output and employment in the short run, and causes a deterioration in the trade balance.

Without complete sterilization, of course, as long as the trade account is out of balance, the money supply will be changing. As with exchange rate changes, the magnitude of the total change in the money supply indirectly induced by the change in government expenditures must be of such a magnitude that $(dB/d\gamma) + (dB/dm)(dm/d\gamma) = 0$. If $dB/d\gamma < 0$ and $dB/dm < 0$, then $dm/d\gamma < 0$ also. Denoting $dm/d\gamma$ by ξ, and solving the model for the long-run effect of an expansionary "buy domestic" policy on the level of output and

---

[11] The assumption that the Marshall-Lerner condition is met is retained throughout the remainder of this chapter.

employment yields

$$(4.32) \qquad \frac{dY}{d\gamma} = \frac{1}{\Delta_3}\left(1 + \xi \frac{D_i}{L_i}\right).$$

Since $\xi < 0$, the sign of dY/dm appears to be indeterminate. However, if equation (4.31) and equation (4.3) multiplied by ξ are added together, then it is readily established that $[1 + \xi(D_i/L_i)] > 0$, so that $dY/d\gamma > 0$.

This result can be shown graphically and is, perhaps, easier to explain intuitively in a diagrammatic context. To do this, note first that, insofar as impact effects are concerned, shifts in the aggregate demand and external balance curves are

$$(4.33) \qquad \frac{dY^d}{d\gamma} = \frac{1}{\Delta_1} > 0$$

and

$$(4.34) \qquad \frac{dY^B}{d\gamma} = 0.$$

That is, the impact effect of the autonomous increase in government expenditures on the domestically produced good is to shift the aggregate demand curve for the domestically produced good to the right, while leaving the (short-run) external balance line unchanged. In Figure 4.9, this moves the economy from point A to point E. However, at E, a trade deficit has emerged, and the nominal money supply is falling. From equations (4.14) and (4.15), it is clear that this drop in the money supply shifts the demand curve to the left, while it also shifts the external balance line to the right. Thus, their new common intersection will be at a point like point C in Figure 4.9.

Intuitively, this result is quite appealing. In the short run, the exogenous increase in demand raises output and the income (real and money) of domestic residents. Via the usual multiplier effects, this leads to increased expenditures on both foreign

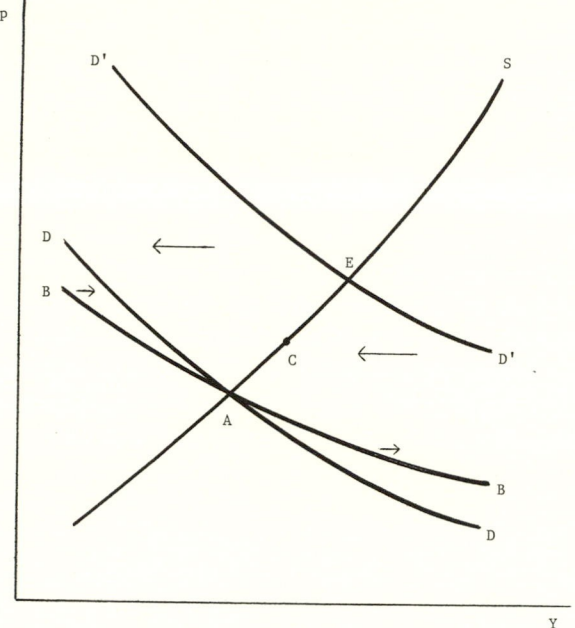

Figure 4.9

and domestic goods. When the new short-run equilibrium is reached, domestic output, income, and imports all are higher. Since the price of the domestic good also is higher, (or, at best unchanged if the economy were in the extreme Keynesian range of the aggregate supply function), exports are lower (or, at best unchanged) and there is a deficit in the balance of trade.

With a trade deficit, the money supply begins to decline. As it declines, interest rates rise, cutting back domestic spending on both the domestic good and the imported good, and reducing the trade deficit. Note, however, that equilibrium cannot be at the old level of prices and income. With a permanently lower nominal stock of money, the old level of prices and income would also be characterized by a higher interest rate. However, at the old level of prices and income but a higher

139

interest rate there would, as long as $F_i < 0$, be a lower level of imports. Since exports are, by assumption, not affected, there would also be a trade surplus. Therefore, the new long-run equilibrium, where trade is balanced, will have to be at a higher level of output and income, in order to induce a higher level of imports.

The conclusion that fiscal policy is expansionary, however, is based on the assumption that none of the exogenous increase in government spending is on the imported good. If this assumption is relaxed, then the interesting result emerges that fiscal policy can be completely ineffective in raising the level of employment and output. This can be readily established with the aid of the diagrammatic aperatus already constructed. By way of preliminaries, note that

$$(4.35) \qquad \frac{dY^B}{d\zeta} = -\frac{1}{\Delta_2},$$

where, as before, $\Delta_2 = F_y - (F_i/L_i) L_{\bar{Y}}$. By assumption $\Delta_2 > 0$, and, therefore $dY^B/d\zeta < 0$. This says nothing more than that an autonomous increase in demand for the imported good tends to generate a trade deficit. Since $dY^d/d\gamma > 0$, $d\gamma > 0$ and $d\zeta > 0$ imply that the aggregate demand and external balance curves shift as in Figure 4.10. Since the resulting deficit will cause the stock of nominal money to fall, thus shifting the external balance line to the right and the aggregate demand curve to the left, a sufficient condition for fiscal policy to have no long-run impact on the level of output and employment is that the magnitudes of $d\gamma$ and $d\zeta$ be such that

$$\left|\frac{dY^B}{d\zeta}\right| = \left|\frac{dY^d}{d\gamma}\right|, \quad \text{and that} \quad \left|\frac{dY^d}{dm}\right| = \left|\frac{dY^B}{dm}\right|.$$

Obviously, this is a fairly stringent condition. However, it is not the only condition under which fiscal policy would be ineffective. As long as the magnitudes of the shifts in the

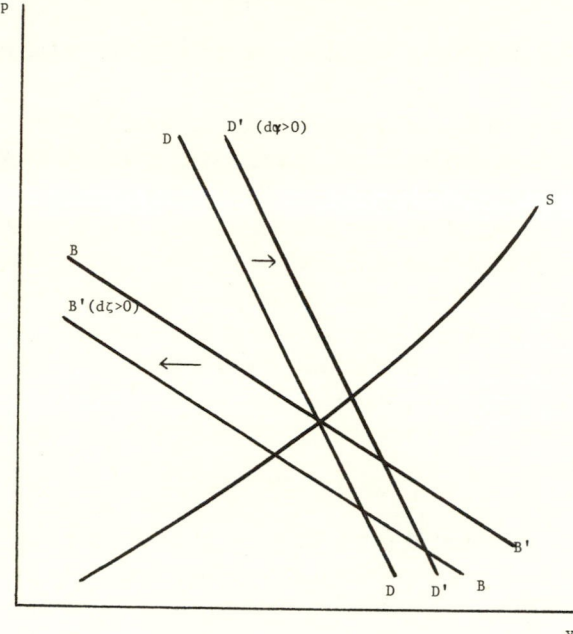

Figure 4.10

external balance and aggregate demand curves with respect to an expansionary fiscal policy are such that they are just counterbalanced by the shifts in the same curves with respect to the resultant change in the money supply, fiscal policy will be ineffective. And, in general, as long as the government does not follow a "buy domestic" policy, the expansionary effect of any given increase in total expenditure will be reduced, or perhaps reversed, in the long run. In the extreme (and extremely unlikely) case where $dy = 0$ while $d\zeta > 0$, the "expansionary" fiscal policy will always have a net contractionary effect on the economy.

141

Appendix: Mathematical Derivations

SINCE the long-run results presented are obtained by introducing a modification to the basic model developed in Chapter 3 then solving the model in exactly the same way, and since the derivations of the equations found in Chapter 3 are discussed in considerable detail in the mathematical appendix to that chapter, the exact derivations of the results found in Chapter 4 will not be discussed in great detail. Rather, the exact nature of the modifications will be given, and the method of solution merely indicated.

THE LONG-RUN MODELS

As the text indicated, in the long run the money supply becomes an endogenous variable in the economy unless the monetary authorities can succeed in completely sterilizing the monetary effects of a balance of payments surplus or deficit. Starting from a point of balanced trade, and imposing the requirement that trade be balanced as a condition of long-run equilibrium, permits a comparative static examination of the long-run effects of a change in a control variable. Insofar as the nominal money supply is concerned, it was noted that it is sufficient to incorporate the additional equation $dm/de = \rho$ into the set of totally differentiated equations of the model. To incorporate fiscal policy, the shift parameters γ and ζ are added to the functions giving domestic demand for the domestic good and import demand, respectively. In this case, the long-run Keynesian system reduces to

$$(4A.1) \quad \begin{bmatrix} 1 - D_y + \beta(D_{eq} - X_{p/e}) & -D_i \\ L_{\bar{Y}} + \beta(\alpha m + (1 - \alpha)yL_{\bar{Y}}) & L_i \end{bmatrix} \begin{bmatrix} dY \\ d_i \end{bmatrix}$$

$$= \begin{bmatrix} D_{eq} - X_{p/e} & 1 & 0 \\ \rho - (1 - \alpha)(1 - \mu)m & \xi & \xi^* \end{bmatrix} \begin{bmatrix} de \\ dy \\ d\zeta \end{bmatrix}$$

where $\xi = dm/dy$ and $\xi^* = dm/d\zeta$, and $\xi, \xi^* < 0$.

The Classical system, on the other hand, reduces to

$$(4A.2) \qquad [A] \begin{bmatrix} dY \\ di \end{bmatrix} = \begin{bmatrix} 0 & 1 & 0 \\ \rho - m & \xi & \xi^* \end{bmatrix} \begin{bmatrix} de \\ dy \\ d\zeta \end{bmatrix}$$

where A is the same as the left-hand side coefficient matrix in equations (4A.1), except that, as usual, θ replaces β.

Macroeconomic versus Walrasian
Models of an Open Economy

IN THE preceding chapters, Keynesian and Classical versions of a macroeconomic income-expenditure model have been employed to examine the response of employment, output, and the balance of trade to changes in various control variables. One justification for using this conceptual framework, aside from a desire to provide a model fully integrating the elasticities and absorption approaches to payments analysis, is that perusal of the payments literature reveals that the principal tool employed in general (more or less) equilibrium analyses of the adjustment process has been some version of an open-economy macroeconomic model. However, in this perusal, the reader also will find a small—but growing—number of authors who, following Hahn (1959), have attacked balance of payments problems using Walrasian-type models modified to include money.[1] That this latter approach has not been as popular as the former, at least until relatively recently, is the result of several factors, the most important of which seem to be (1) the historic tendency to think of balance of payments problems as "macroeconomic" and (2) the objection of many monetary theorists to the use of a Walrasian framework for monetary analysis.[2]

---

[1] The macroeconomic category includes (somewhat arbitrarily, perhaps) such monetarist analyses as those of Mundell (1968), Dornbush (1971), Johnson (1972), and Frenkel and Rodriquez (1975), while such monetarist papers as those of Kemp (1970), Dornbush (1973b), and Krueger (1974) are classified as Walrasian in orientation.

[2] Clower (1965, 1967), Hahn (1965), Herschleifer (1973), Leijonhufvud (1968), and others have argued that a Walrasian framework is conceptually inap-

Yet, as was demonstrated in the previous chapter, results originally obtained in a Walras-Hahn framework appear again in the Classical version of the macroeconomic income-expenditure model, as well as in macroeconomic versions of the monetarist model. This suggests that, in spite of some underlying conceptual differences, the two approaches may have more in common than generally has been assumed. In any event, the appearance of common results suggests that a more careful examination of the structural similarities and differences in the Walrasian and macroeconomic approaches is in order. Moreover, since the role of nontraded, or home, goods in the payments adjustment process is more easily handled in a Walrasian setting, such an examination seems essential if these results are to be compared with more macroeconomic ones. By examining the structures of both the Walrasian and macroeconomic models, this chapter provides at least part of the framework within which such a comparison can be made.

Before proceeding, it should be emphasized that no position is taken here as to the relative merits of a Walrasian model with money or on the issue of whether or not the "Keynesian" model developed in the preceding chapter adequately reflects the economics of Keynes.[3] While these controversies in the literature are both important and interesting, they are not considered here. The aim of this chapter is the more modest one of providing a comparison of the structures of two traditional

propriate for analyses of monetary economics because the logical structure of the model obviates the need for money as a medium of exchange. Since the medium of exchange function of money is viewed as essential by these authors, they argue that a model without it is not a monetary one.

[3] While the "Keynesian" model of Chapters 3 and 4 does not capture the role of expectations discussed by Keynes, nor the "disequilibrium" problems stressed by many current neo-Keynesians, it does seem to avoid the Clower criticism of Walrasian models in that the specification of the model in Chapters 3 and 4 does not require that a "barter" model underly the "real" portion. Thus, money does have a role to play.

approaches to payments analyses, taking at face value whatever explicit or implicit theoretical arguments are employed to justify the two types of models.

The rest of this chapter is divided into three sections. The first compares the money market specifications of the Walrasian system with the macroeconomic one developed and used in Chapters 3 and 4. This comparison identifies the reason for the qualitative similarities between Kemp's[4] results on the (short-run/sterilized) effects of exchange rate and money supply changes and those obtained in Chapter 4's discussion of the Classical version of the macroeconomic model. In the process of this comparison, the Hahn-Kemp results are generalized to allow for a bond market, and the role of nontraded goods in the adjustment process is (briefly) examined. The second section relaxes the Walrasian model's assumption of fixed factor supplies. This modified model is then used to examine the behavior of this system under conditions of neo-Keynesian less than full employment. Section III comments on the overall similarities and differences between the two approaches.

I   WALRAS-HAHN OPEN-ECONOMY MODELS

The Basic Model

The essential structure of the model used in Hahn-type studies of open economies should be well known to anyone familiar with the traditional analysis of pure exchange economies. However, in the open-economy monetary model, instead of a simple two-good, two-country model, extra dimensions are added to the analysis by introducing what is essentially a third

---

[4] As was noted in Chapter 3, others (e.g. Dornbush 1973b, Frenkel and Rodriguez 1975, and Krueger 1974) also have obtained this result. Since Kemp appears to have been the first to present it publicly, however, it is referred to throughout this chapter as the Kemp result, or Kemp's theorem.

commodity in each country, namely home-country fiat money. (In models of the trade account, it is assumed that residents of each country only hold units of their own country's currency.) The model also can be interpreted as including a production sector, with output (supply) of each good given by a standard neoclassical production function that has two primary factors, capital and labor, as its arguments. The phrase "can be interpreted" is inserted because the model in fact is developed in terms of neoclassical excess demand functions. This development is both its major strength and its main weakness. It is an advantage because it reduces an otherwise exceedingly complex mathematical structure to a relatively small number of equations, thus making analytical solutions of the system practical. At times this is a disadvantage because the results can be taken as coming from almost any underlying structure desired, which means that their usefulness to the policy maker depends critically on his ability to give them a reasonable economic interpretation.[5] This point will be returned to and developed at greater length in section II.

If a barter model of a trading world is considered—and it is assumed that there are two countries, each producing two goods (both of which are traded internationally) under perfectly competitive conditions, with primary factors of production in perfectly inelastic supply—then the excess demand-function formulation of the model is exceedingly simple. Under these assumptions, both demand functions and supply functions depend only on the relative prices of the two goods. Obviously, therefore, the excess demand functions also depend only on the prices of the two goods, and are zero-degree homogeneous in these two arguments. In this case, the only

---

[5] Kemp (1970) even has gone so far as to demonstrate that a two-good, two-country model in fact can be interpreted as a three-good (two traded, one nontraded), two-country model with very little effort.

thing to be determined is the terms of trade. This follows from the structure of the model, which can be expressed as follows:

$$
\begin{aligned}
E_1(p_1, p_2) + E_1^* \left(\frac{p_1}{e}, \frac{p_2}{e} \right) &= 0 \\
E_2(p_1, p_2) + E_2^* \left(\frac{p_1}{e}, \frac{p_2}{e} \right) &= 0
\end{aligned}
$$
(5.1)

where: p_i = the "price" of the ith good (these are accounting prices, in Country 1's unit of account),

E_i = excess demand for the ith good,

e = "exchange rate" (assumed fixed),

and where asterisks are now used to denote foreign country variables.

Before proceeding further, the reader is warned that, in order (hopefully) to keep the notation as simple as possible, there are some departures from the notational conventions of the previous three chapters. In addition to using asterisks to denote foreign country variables, the first subscript on a symbol is now used to denote the good to which that symbol refers. Thus, E_1 and p_1 refer to the excess demand and price for the first good, respectively. Later, where functions are differentiated, the *second* subscript will be used to denote the argument with respect to which the partial derivative has been taken. Wherever possible, however, the same letter will be used to denote a quantity (N = labor, for example) or functional relationship. An explicit exception here is the demand for money function, where the L, or liquidity, notation will be dropped because it is too identified with a macroeconomic model structure.

With this in mind, equations (5.1) require that total world supply of the two goods equals total world demand. However, each country faces a budget constraint of the form

(5.2) $p_1 E_1 + p_2 E_2 = 0$ (for country 1, say).

Substituting from equations (5.1) into equation (5.2) yields

$$(5.3) \qquad -p_1 E_1^* \left(\frac{p_1}{e}, \frac{p_2}{e} \right) - p_2 E_2^* \left(\frac{p_1}{e}, \frac{p_2}{e} \right) = 0.$$

Since the E_i are homogeneous, however, this immediately reduces to

$$(5.3a) \qquad -E_1^* \left(\frac{p_2}{p_1} \right) - \frac{p_2}{p_1} E_2^* \left(\frac{p_2}{p_1} \right) = 0.$$

Equation (5.3a), which clearly is a function only of the relative price p_2/p_1, implies that balanced trade is an equilibrium condition in the model. Since the Walrasian *tâtonnement* process is the assumed adjustment mechanism, this means that trade is always balanced in this system.

The Model with Money

It is this basic model that Hahn (1959), Kemp (1970), Dornbush (1973b), and others have modified by incorporating money. While the exact details of the various models differ somewhat, in general they all tend to follow Patinkin in the formulation of the money demand function and the accompanying revisions in the demand functions for goods. Specifically, it is assumed that individual utility maximizers have a desired stock of money. This desired stock is a function of the money prices of the goods in the system, and the level of wealth (in this case existing money balances), and is assumed to be homogeneous of degree one in the arguments. In a two-commodity framework, this gives a home-country equation of the form

$$(5.4) \qquad m^d = m^d(p_1, p_2, W)$$

where m^d is the desired stock of fiat money, the p_i are now the money prices of the two goods, and W is the level of net wealth. As with the other equations of the model, (5.4) is an aggregate of the implied individual functions. If m^s is the exogenous supply of fiat money, then equation (5.4) and the exogenous supply imply an excess demand function of the form

$$(5.5) \qquad E_m = E_m(p_1, p_2, W, m^s),$$

where $E_m = m^d - m^s$. However, since money is the only asset in this model, $W = m$, and since the money supply must be held, $m = m^s$, so the excess demand function can be written as

$$(5.5a) \qquad E_m = E_m(p_1, p_2, m).$$

Equation (5.5a) is assumed to be homogeneous of degree one in m and the p_i. Using the notation E_{ij} to denote the partial derivative of the ith excess demand function with respect to the jth argument of the function, it is assumed that $E_{mj} > 0$, $j = 1, 2$, while $E_{mm} < 0$. This says merely that all goods are assumed to be gross substitutes for money, and that an increase in the supply of fiat money reduces the excess demand for fiat money. (This latter assumption—i.e. $E_{mm} < 0$—also implies that the effect of an increase in wealth is to increase the demand for money balances in smaller proportion. In other words, it assumes that $0 \leqq \partial m^d/\partial W < 1$).

With money introduced into the model, the demand for goods equations must be modified. This is done by assuming that goods demand depends on the level of wealth as well as on the money prices of the two goods. Since supply still depends only on the goods prices, the excess demand functions become

$$(5.6) \qquad E_i = E_i(p_1, p_2, m), \quad i = 1, 2.$$

Equation (5.6) is zero-degree homogeneous in the p_i and m. A set of equations analogous to (5.5a) and (5.6) is also assumed to hold for the foreign country.

With the introduction of money, the budget constraint must be modified to read

$$(5.6a) \qquad p_1 E_1 + p_2 E_2 + E_m = 0.$$

If it is assumed that commodity 1 is imported while commodity 2 is exported, then, using equation (5.2a), the balance of trade in units of the domestic currency is given by

$$(5.7) \qquad B = -(p_1 E_1 + p_2 E_2) = E_m.$$

From equation (5.7) it is obvious that if desired and actual money stocks are equal, trade is balanced.

The entire model now consists of two equations stating the requirement that world demand for each good equals world supply. To this is appended either equation (5.7) or an equivalent expression giving the trade balance in units of the foreign currency.[6] This then gives three equations that are sufficient to determine the two money prices and the trade balance (with the exchange rate and money supply taken as exogenous). Making use of the excess demand functions (5.6), the model consists of

$$E_1(p_1, p_2, m) + E_1^* \left(\frac{p_1}{e}, \frac{p_2}{e}, m^* \right) = 0$$

$$(5.8) \qquad E_2(p_1, p_2, m) + E_2^* \left(\frac{p_1}{e}, \frac{p_2}{e}, m^* \right) = 0$$

$$E_m(p_1, p_2, m) - B = 0.$$

Totally differentiating equations (5.8) and rearranging yields

$$(5.9) \qquad \begin{bmatrix} E_{11} + E_{11}^* & E_{12} + E_{12}^* & 0 \\ E_{21} + E_{21}^* & E_{22} + E_{22}^* & 0 \\ E_{m1} & E_{m2} & -1 \end{bmatrix} \begin{bmatrix} dp_1 \\ dp_2 \\ dB \end{bmatrix}$$

$$= - \begin{bmatrix} mE_{1m} & m^* E_{1m}^* & -(E_{11}^* + E_{12}^*) \\ mE_{2m} & m^* E_{2m}^* & -(E_{21}^* + E_{22}^*) \\ mE_{mm} & 0 & 0 \end{bmatrix} \begin{bmatrix} dm/m \\ dm^*/m^* \\ de/e \end{bmatrix}.$$

[6] Equation (5.5) is dropped from the complete model via Walras' Law.

151

However, from the homogeneity properties of the system,

$$- \sum_{j=1}^{2} E_{ij}^* = m^* E_{im}^*.$$

Substituting into the right-hand side of equations (5.9), and denoting the coefficient matrix on the left-hand side by A then yields

$$(5.10) \quad [A] \begin{bmatrix} dp_1 \\ dp_2 \\ dB \end{bmatrix}$$

$$= - \begin{bmatrix} mE_{1m} & m^*E_{1m}^* & m^*E_{1m}^* \\ mE_{2m} & m^*E_{2m}^* & m^*E_{2m}^* \\ mE_{mm} & 0 & 0 \end{bmatrix} \begin{bmatrix} dm/m \\ dm^*/m^* \\ de/e \end{bmatrix}.$$

From (5.10) it is immediately obvious that $dB/(de/e) = dB/(dm^*/m^*)$. Using (5.10), the homogeneity properties of the system (in particular that $mE_{mm} + \sum_{j=1}^{2} E_{mj} = E_m$), and the fact that trade is initially balanced, so that $E_m = 0$, together with considerable algebra, also will yield the result[7] that $dB/(de/e) = -dB/(dm/m)$.

Walrasian versus Macroeconomic Results

Of interest here, more than the actual result, is the mechanism at work. From equations (5.10) it is apparent that both a devaluation and a change in the money supply exert an influence on the economy via Patinkin's real-balance effect. That is, with the homogeneity properties of the system, changes in either the nominal money supply or the exchange rate have an effect only because they lead to a change in real wealth. This change in wealth then leads to a change in demand for the various goods.

[7] See Chapter 4 for a fuller discussion of Kemp's theorem.

To compare this mechanism with the one at work in the Classical version of the aggregate model discussed in Chapters 3 and 4, note first that the demand equations in that system can be transformed so as to look much like the excess demand equations (5.6a). Converting equation (3.7) [i.e. $m/\Phi = L(y/\Phi, i)$] to an expression giving the interest rate as a function of m/Φ and y/Φ, or, more generally, as a function of p, eq, y, and m, and substituting this expression into equation (3.4) yields

$$(5.11) \qquad D = D(y, p, eq, i(y, p, eq, m)) = \tilde{D}(y, p, eq, m)$$

where now the tilde over the functional notation denotes a reduced-form equation. A similar expression obviously would result if this were done for equation (3.5) also. But notice that, in this case, any change in D following from a change in m is the result, not of a wealth or real-balance effect, but rather of a change in the interest rate following from the money supply change. When the effects of exchange rate and money supply changes are traced through the entire system, it becomes clear that equiproportional changes in each of them have identical effects on the economy because they have an equal effect on the interest rate.

The fact that, in Chapter 4's aggregate Classical system, changes in the money supply and exchange rate influence the economy via their impact on the interest rate rather than via a real-balance effect is significant because it implies that, in that model, an equiproportional change in the supply of bonds has the same impact on the target variables.[8] In the Walrasian system, however, the introduction of bonds and a rate of

---

[8] It should be pointed out that it is not necessary to include a real-balance effect in the aggregate model of Chapters 3 and 4. As has been pointed out by Johnson (1967), if all money is inside money there will be no aggregate real-balance effect. Also, there is no reason to assume that the disaggregated general equilibrium model lying behind the aggregate one is a Walrasian barter system.

interest means that equiproportional changes in the exchange rate and money supply no longer have the same effect on the economy.

This can be seen by extending the Walras-Hahn-Kemp model. To do this, assume that there are government bonds (in the form of consols) in the system. When these are included, the logic of the model suggests that, analogous to the stock of money, there is a desired stock of bonds, which is a function of the prices of all goods in the system and the level of net wealth. If g = government bonds, this desired stock is given by

$$(5.12) \qquad g^d = g^d(p_g, p_1, p_2, W)$$

where g^d is the desired stock of bonds, p_g is the price of a bond ($p_g = 1/i$), and all other notation is as before.[9] If g^s is the supply of bonds (= the amount held by individuals), then equation (5.12) can be converted to an excess demand function of the form

$$(5.13) \qquad E_g = E_g(p_g, p_1, p_2, W, g)$$

where $E_g = g^d - g^s$, $W = G + m$, and where $G = p_g g$ = the nominal value of the stock of bonds held. With bonds in the system, the excess demand for money must be rewritten as

$$(5.14) \qquad E_m = E_m(p_g, p_1, p_2, W, m)$$

and the excess demand for goods as

$$(5.15) \qquad E_i = E_i(p_g, p_1, p_2, W); \quad i = 1, 2.$$

Similar relationships are assumed to hold for the foreign country.

If the bonds of each country are held only by the residents of that country (i.e. if there are no capital flows), then the price

---

[9] Of course, net wealth now consists of both money and bonds, so that $W = p_g g + m$.

of bonds can differ in each country and the complete model consists of a set of four equations

$$(5.16) \quad \begin{aligned} E_1(p_g, p_1, p_2, W) + E_1^*\left(p_g^*, \frac{p_1}{e}, \frac{p_2}{e}, W^*\right) &= 0 \\ E_2(\quad \cdot \quad) + E_2^*(\quad \cdot \quad) &= 0 \\ E_G(p_g, p_1, p_2, W, g) &= 0 \\ E_G^*\left(p_g^*, \frac{p_1}{e}, \frac{p_2}{e}, W^*, g^*\right) &= 0 \end{aligned}$$

and the definition of the balance of trade, equation (5.7).[10] (Each function denoted by ($\cdot$) has as its arguments the same variables as the function above it.

This introduction of bonds into the analysis implies that equiproportional changes in the exchange rate and money supply no longer have equal impacts on the targets variables in the system.[11] Since the complete model proves to be rather complicated, it is solved here only for the small-country case. However, even this special case provides insights into the adjustment process. In addition, the results obtained can be directly compared with the small-country results presented in Chapter 3.

Under the assumption that the home country is small, the complete model can be reduced to a system of two equations,

---

[10] If only domestic residents hold domestic bonds, the bond market must be in equilibrium in each country. From the budget constraint, this implies that the net trade balance still equals the excess demand for money. To see this, observe that the budget constraint now becomes $p_g E_g + p_1 E_1 + p_2 E_2 + E_m = 0$. The trade balance is $B = -(p_1 E_1 + p_2 E_2)$, so the budget constraint can be written as $p_g E_g - B + E_m = 0$. But $E_g = 0$ from equations (5.16).

[11] A minor additional problem that arises is that the usual comparative statics type analysis of this system cannot be undertaken without making use of an extensive stability analysis of the model. This is because the usual set of assumptions on the signs of the various partial derivatives are insufficient to guarantee a sign to the determinant of the comparative statics system.

155

instead of the five equations it takes to describe the general case. Since the home country is small, it cannot affect the real terms of trade. Thus, the relative prices of goods 1 and 2 do not change, and, by the Hicks composite-good theorem, they can be aggregated and treated as a single traded good. Since the rest of the world is effectively ignored in a small-country analysis, the equation determining E_G^* can be dropped. This leaves a two-equation system of the form

$$(5.17) \quad \begin{aligned} E_g(p_g, p_1, W, g) &= 0 \\ B + p_1 E_1(p_g, p_1, W) &= 0 \end{aligned}$$

where E_1 now is the excess demand for the (composite) traded good, and p_1 is its domestic price. From the small-country assumption, $p_1 = e p_1^*$, where p_1^* is the world price of the traded good ($=$ the terms of trade). By the small-country assumption p_1^* is a constant.

By totally differentiating equations (5.17), and making use of the homogeneity properties of the model and the assumptions that, initially, trade is balanced and all prices and the exchange rate are equal to unity, the differentiated system can be reduced to

$$(5.18) \quad \begin{bmatrix} E_{g0} & 0 \\ E_{10} & 1 \end{bmatrix} \begin{bmatrix} dp_g \\ dB \end{bmatrix}$$
$$= -\begin{bmatrix} E_{g1} & WE_{gW} & E_{gg} \\ E_1 + E_{11} & WE_{1W} & 0 \end{bmatrix} \begin{bmatrix} de \\ dW \\ dg \end{bmatrix}$$

where $E_{i0} = \partial E_i / \partial p_g$, $E_{i1} = \partial E_i / \partial p_1$, $E_{1W} = \partial E_1 / \partial W$, and $E_{ig} = \partial E_i / \partial g$, for $i = g, 1$. However, $dW = dm + p_g \, dg + g \, dp_g$, and $E_{gg} = -1$, while the homogeneity properties of the system imply that $E_{g1} + WE_{gW} + gE_{gg} = E_g$ and $E_{11} + WE_{1W} = 0$. Since $E_1 = 0$ by the assumption of initially balanced trade, while $E_g = 0$ in equilibrium, equations (5.18) can be written as

$$(5.19) \quad \begin{bmatrix} \tilde{E}_{g0} & 0 \\ \tilde{E}_{10} & 1 \end{bmatrix} \begin{bmatrix} dp_g \\ dB \end{bmatrix}$$

$$= - \begin{bmatrix} -[(GE_{gW} - g) + mE_{gW}] & mE_{gW} & GE_{gW} - g \\ -(G + m)E_{1W} & mE_{1W} & GE_{1W} \end{bmatrix} \begin{bmatrix} de/e \\ dm/m \\ dg/g \end{bmatrix}$$

where $\tilde{E}_{i0} = E_{i0} + gE_{iW}$, $i = g, 1$ and $G = p_g g$. From equations (5.19) it is immediately obvious that $|dB/(de/e)| \neq |dB/(dm/m)|$. Explicitly solving for the change in the trade balance when either the exchange rate or the money supply are altered yields

$$(5.20) \quad \frac{dB}{dm/m} = -\frac{m}{\Delta} \{E_{1W}\tilde{E}_{g0} - E_{gW}\tilde{E}_{10}\} < 0$$

and

$$(5.21) \quad \frac{dB}{de/e} = \frac{1}{\Delta} \{m[E_{1W}\tilde{E}_{g0} - E_{gW}\tilde{E}_{10}]$$

$$+ G[E_{1W}\tilde{E}_{g0} + (1 - E_{gW})\tilde{E}_{10}]\}$$

where $\Delta = \tilde{E}_{g0} < 0.$[12]

A comparison of equations (5.20) and (5.21) reveals that the introduction of bonds has generated several changes in the system. First, it is no longer guaranteed that a devaluation will improve the balance of trade. Since $E_{gW} < 1$ (but positive) as long as E_{mW} and E_{1W} are positive, it is possible that the sign of dB/de will be negative. Second, the expression for $dB/(de/e)$ is composed of two parts: (i) $-dB/(dm/m)$ and (ii) terms reflecting the impact of the devaluation on the bond market. Third,

---

[12] It has been assumed that $E_{g0} < 0$, while $E_{10} > 0$. Since $\tilde{E}_{g0} = E_{g0} + gE_{gW}$, and $E_{g0} < 0$ while $E_{gW} > 0$, assuming that $\tilde{E}_{g0} < 0$ is equivalent to assuming that bonds are a normal good, with the substitution effects of a price change dominating the wealth effects.

if there are no interest rate effects in the goods market (i.e. if $E_{10} = 0$), then a devaluation always improves the trade balance, and $|dB/(de/e)| > |dB/(dm/m)|$, i.e. in the absence of interest rate effects in the goods market a devaluation is a more powerful tool for correcting a deficit than is a contraction in the money supply. If, on the other hand, there are interest rate effects, then even if a devaluation improves the trade balance (i.e. even if $dB/de > 0$), whether or not $|dB/(de/e)| > |dB/(dm/m)|$ will depend on whether of not $|E_{1w}\tilde{E}_{g0}| < |(1 - E_{gw})\tilde{E}_{10}|$.

Fortunately, all of these changes can be given a straightforward heuristic explanation. In the system described here, any change in the exchange rate operates by changing the real value of assets—i.e. it operates via a wealth effect. A devaluation lowers the real value of bond and money holdings, which in turn leads to a change in the demand for goods and assets. In addition, a change occurs in the price of goods and bonds, but this is the indirect result of the demand shifts caused by the wealth effect. If goods demand does not depend on bond prices (or, equivalently, on interest rates), the direct wealth effects are the end of the story. In this case, since money and bonds each constitute only a fraction of total wealth, and since changes in their nominal quantities operate via a wealth effect, it is obvious that a change in either of them can affect the trade balance with only a fraction of the impact of an equiproportional change in the exchange rate.

When interest rate changes have an effect on goods demand, the situation becomes more complex. A change in the supply of bonds affects the level of wealth directly, via the change in the quantity of bonds outstanding, and indirectly, via a change in their price. In this case, the direct quantity effects work in an opposite direction from the indirect price effect—one tending to increase a trade deficit, and the other tending to decrease it. Put another way, any change in the quantity of bonds affects the level of nominal wealth in two ways: first it affects the number of units of bonds constituting total wealth, and, second, it affects the money price of those units. When money is the only asset in the system, on the other hand, a change in the supply of money can only alter the number of units of money making up wealth. Since money is the numeraire, by definition there cannot be a "price effect" (i.e. a change in the money price of money) accompanying the quantity change.

Despite this assymmetry, it is still true that equiproportional changes in the exchange rate and in both components of total wealth together will have equal impacts on the balance of trade. That is, solving for $dB/(dg/g)$ yields

$$(5.22) \qquad \frac{dB}{dg/g} = -\frac{1}{\Delta} \{G[E_{1W}\tilde{E}_{g0} + (1 - E_{gW})\tilde{E}_{10}]\}.$$

From equations (5.20), (5.21), and (5.22) it is obvious that $dB/(de/e) = -|dB/(dm/m) + dB/(dg/g)|$, with, now, the sign of $dB/(de/e)$ indeterminate a priori.

Thus, a principal monetarist theorem, which was seen in Chapter 4 to be a general result in a small-country, money-bonds macroeconomic model without a wealth effect, is seen to be a special case in a Walrasian model, valid only in the absence of an alternate financial asset.[13]

In light of the ambiguity in the sign of $dB/(dg/g)$ and, for that matter, $dB/(de/e)$, it is impossible to draw an unambiguous implication for trade policy from these results. If, however, as seems likely it is generally true that $dB/(dg/g) < 0$ (i.e. that an increase in the supply of bonds has the effect of inducing a trade deficit), then a clear-cut policy implication results. In this case $dB/de > 0$ always, and the exchange rate becomes

---

[13] Of course, as was already demonstrated in Appendix B to Chapter 3, the Kemp theorem does not carry through to a two-country macroeconomic framework with both money and bonds.

an unambiguously more powerful policy tool than changes in either the money supply or supply of bonds alone (as already noted, this follows immediately if $\tilde{E}_{10} = 0$). Moreover, the exchange rate is a more useful tool in that it is clearly easier to change it by, say, 10 percent than to change the nominal stock of money outstanding by 20 percent or more. On the other hand, if $dB/(dg/g) < 0$ is not insured, then a change in the money supply has the virtue of being unambiguous in terms of its effect on the trade balance.

The Role of Nontraded Goods

Kemp (1970) has shown that the standard two-good, two-country model with money can be reinterpreted as a three-good, two-country model as long as one of the three goods in each country is a purely home, or nontraded, one, given some assumptions on the derivatives of the excess demand functions. This somewhat surprising conclusion turns out to be easily verifiable from the homogeneity properties of the system. Unfortunately, this proposition is no longer valid when bonds are introduced into the system; however, it can be reestablished with one additional (and not unreasonable) assumption. To see this, assume the existence of a third, nontraded, good in each country. This implies that all excess demand functions for commodities are of the form

$$(5.23) \qquad E_i = E_i(p_g, p_1, p_2, p_3, W), \quad i = 1, 2, 3$$

while excess demands for assets are of the form

$$(5.24) \qquad E_i = E_i(p_g, p_1, p_2, p_3, W, i), \quad i = g, m.$$

For the foreign country, equivalent asterisked expressions are assumed to hold. However, since the third good in each country is nontraded, $E_3 = 0 = E_3^*$, and the two implicit functions can be solved explicitly for p_3 and p_3^*, and the resulting expressions substituted into the remaining equations.

If, following Hahn (1959), Kemp (1962, 1970), Krueger (1974), and others, it is assumed that (1) all commodities are weak gross substitutes, so that $E_{ij} > 0$, $i, j = 1, 2, 3, i \neq j$; (2) all commodities are gross substitutes for money and bonds so that $E_{mj}, E_{gj} > 0, j = 1, 2, 3$; (3) all marginal propensities to spend out of wealth are positive, so that $E_{iW} > 0, i = 1, 2, 3$; and (4) excess demands are negatively related to the interest rate, so that $E_{i0} > 0, i = 1, 2, 3, m$ in the unreduced functions, then the same will be true in the reduced functions where p_3 and p_3^* have been solved out of the system.

In the reduced system, all commodity excess demand functions are of the form

$$(5.25) \qquad \tilde{E}_i = E_i(p_g, p_1, p_2, p_3(p_g, p_1, p_2, W), W),$$

while both asset excess demand functions are of the form

$$(5.25a) \qquad \tilde{E}_i = \tilde{E}_i(p_g, p_1, p_2, p_3(p_g, p_1, p_2, W), W, i)$$

$$i = g, m.$$

From the fact that $E_3(\cdot) = 0$ it follows by the implicit function theorem that

$$(5.26) \qquad dp_3 = -\frac{1}{E_{33}} [E_{30} \, dp_g + E_{31} \, dp_1 + E_{32} \, dp_2$$

$$+ E_{3W} \, dW].$$

This implies that

$$(5.27) \qquad \tilde{E}_{ij} = E_{ij} - E_{i3} \frac{E_{3j}}{E_{33.}}, \quad i = 1, 2; \quad j = 0, 1, 2, W.$$

Given the sign assumptions on the derivatives in the unreduced functions, it immediately follows that $\tilde{E}_{ij} > 0$ for $i = 1, 2, g, m$; $j = 0, 1, 2, W, i \neq j$ and $j \neq 0$ if $i = g$. To establish that $E_{ii} < 0$ for $i = 1, 2$, observe that in the unreduced functions the homogeneity properties of the model imply that $-E_{ii} > E_{ij} \geqq 0$. Thus, $0 \leqq -(E_{3j}/E_{33}) < 1$. Since $\tilde{E}_{ii} = E_{ii} - E_{i3}$ (E_{3j}/E_{33}), if $-E_{ii} > E_{i3}$, then $\tilde{E}_{ii} < 0$. Moreover, in the reduced functions $E_{gg} = E_{gg}$ and $\tilde{E}_{mm} = E_{mm}$. This leaves only the sign of $\tilde{E}_{g0}$ undetermined, with $\tilde{E}_{g0} = E_{g0} - E_{g3}(E_{30}/E_{33})$. Unfortunately, since the homogeneity properties of the system imply nothing about interest rate changes (or, equivalently, changes in the price of bonds), the sign of $\tilde{E}_{g0}$ is not determinate without further assumptions. However, since any homogeneity properties of the unreduced functions immediately carry over to the reduced functions, if it is assumed that $\tilde{E}_{g0} < 0$ (i.e. that "direct" price effects dominate cross-price effects), then the reduced form of the model with home goods remains mathematically indistinguishable from equations (5.16).

The significance of this conclusion is that, as long as $\tilde{E}_{g0} < 0$, any result obtained in a two-good framework still can be interpreted as applying to a world where there are nontraded goods. Thus, for example, any conditions necessary and/or sufficient to insure $dB/de > 0$ in the two-good case will apply equally to the home-good situation as well. The only remaining question is the effect of a change in a control variable on relative prices. Krueger (1974) has shown that, for the small-country case, with only money in the model, the price of the home good rises by proportionately less than the increase in the exchange rate. This implies that the relative price of the nontraded good falls. Although not explicitly mentioned by Kemp (who obtained the same result) or Krueger, this fall in its relative price also means that the absolute level of output of the home good falls, while that of the composite traded good rises.[14]

---

[14] This latter proposition follows immediately from the full employment and fixed-factor supplies assumptions of the model. These assumptions mean that the economy is operating along a transformation curve concave to the origin, which in turn means that output of the good whose relative price has fallen also falls.

When bonds are added to the model, it can be shown that this result does not necessarily follow, although it would appear to be the most likely case. Since there are only two effective goods in the model, call p_1 the price of the traded good, while p_3 remains the price of the nontraded good. Then the complete model consists of three equations:

$$E_g(p_g, p_1, p_3, W, g) = 0$$

(5.28) $\qquad E_3(p_g, p_1, p_3, W) = 0$

$$B + p_1 E_1(p_g, p_1, p_3, W) = 0$$

and a definition of $p_1 = ep_1^*$, with p_1^* a constant.

Solving for dp_3 yields

(5.29) $\qquad dp_3 = -\dfrac{E_{31} - \Upsilon E_{g1}}{E_{33} - \Upsilon E_{g3}} \, de$

where $\Upsilon = (E_{30} + gE_{3W})/(E_{g0} + gE_{gW})$. Since Υ and $E_{33} < 0$, while E_{31}, E_{g1}, and $E_{g3} > 0$, it is clear that not even the sign of equation (5.29) is determinate a priori. If $-E_{33} > \Upsilon E_{g3}$, then $dp_3/de > 0$. However, even in this case, $dp_3/p_3 > de/e$ if $E_{31} - \Upsilon E_{g1} > -(E_{33} - \Upsilon E_{g3})$. In both of these cases, however, it is obvious that a failure of the Kemp-Krueger proposition to hold would be the result of unusual interest rate effects. Without bonds in the system, or if the demand for commodities were not responsive to interest rate changes, so that $\Upsilon = 0$, then $dp_3 = -(E_{31}/E_{33}) \, de$, and homogeneity then would imply that $dp_3/p_3 < de/e$.

An Aside on Sterilization

Although there is neither time nor space to examine all the implications here, the model developed above reveals more clearly some of the restrictions on choices of instruments the monetary authorities face if they wish to follow a policy of sterilization. In a closed economy, open-market operations, rediscounting, and changes in reserve requirements all are, in terms of their qualitative effects, equivalent policy instruments. However, in a world of international trade, open-market operations will not, in general, be neutral in their effects. If the monetary authority uses open-market operations to peg the stock of money in domestic hands when there is a balance of payments deficit, it will be purchasing bonds, equal in value to the deficit, from the private sector. However, if the supply of fiat money remains constant while the stock of bonds falls, the price of bonds will be bid up, which implies that the interest rate will fall. Only if there is someone (a banking system, say) willing to supply bonds to the monetary authority at a fixed price can open-market operations be "neutral." And, in the longer term, even this will fail as the supply of bonds is exhausted. In the case of a surplus, the situation is reversed, with the monetary authority selling bonds to absorb money. But, again, this implies that the price of bonds will be changing, or, if demand is infinitely elastic, that the monetary authority's supply ultimately will run out. Similar problems occur with reserve requirements in that changes are bounded by the requirement that reserves lie somewhere between zero and 100 percent. Thus, only rediscounting remains as a perfectly general sterilization tool.

II THE WALRAS-HAHN MODEL WITH UNEMPLOYMENT

With only occasional exceptions, analyses using the Walrasian framework employ the standard neoclassical assumptions of fixed supplies of primary factors of production and full employment. The full-employment assumption is guaranteed by the two assumptions of perfectly flexible money wage rates and prices and of instant costless mobility of factors between industries. As Krueger (1974) has pointed out, however, one can question the need for autonomous monetary policy in a continuously fully employed economy.

What does not seem to be widely recognized, however, is that the model does not have to be interpreted as an extension of the Edgeworth-Bowley box diagram. When presented in its excess-demand function form, it can just as easily be interpreted as describing a world of nonmobile capital specific to each industry (and, in the short run at least, in fixed supply) and mobile labor. As long as production is assumed to take place under competitive conditions with output determined by a standard neoclassical production function, most of the barter theorems will still go through. A model with only labor mobile, in turn, implies that, if a variable labor supply is allowed, the possibility of short-run unemployment can be built into the analysis. Of course, this then means that results obtained in a multigood "Walrasian" framework can be compared with those derived in a more Keynesian setting.

In this section, such an interpretation of the Walras-Hahn model is presented.[15] Since the model with both unemployment and money is rather complex, it is solved explicitly only for the small-country case. This case is sufficient, however, to demonstrate that, even without bonds, the Hahn-Kemp results on the equivalence of exchange rate and money supply changes fail to carry through to a situation of less than full employment in a Walrasian framework, just as they failed to carry through in the macroeconomic one. This is not surprising, of course, since the introduction of the rigidities necessary to generate less than full employment destroys the homogeneity properties of the model necessary to obtain the Hahn-Kemp result.

The Structure of the Basic Model

To see clearly the complexities that the assumption of less than full employment adds to the analysis, it is useful to examine

---

[15] In order to include home goods in the analysis explicitly, and to keep the exposition and solution of the model manageable, bonds are again dropped from the analysis.

the economic structure usually assumed to underlie the excess demand functions of the Walrasian model in more detail. Recall that these functions are generated by assuming that the quantity of each good supplied depends on its own price and the prices of all other goods in the system. If a two-good world is assumed, and the quantity supplied of the ith good is denoted by Q_i^s, this gives a supply function for the ith good of the form

$$(5.30) \qquad Q_i^s = Q_i^s(p_1, p_2), \quad i = 1, 2.$$

It is assumed that equations (5.30) are homogeneous of degree zero in p_1 and p_2, and that $Q_{ij}^s < 0$ for $i, j = 1, 2, i \neq j$, and $Q_{ii}^s > 0$. Demand for each good also depends on the price of all goods in the system, as well as on money income and, in a monetary model, on the existing stock of money. Denoting the quantity demanded of the ith good as Q_i^d, this gives the demand functions

$$(5.31) \qquad Q_i^d = Q_i^d(p_1, p_2, y, m), \quad i = 1, 2$$

where y is money income. However, since money income is merely the value of aggregate output (i.e. $y = p_1 Q_1^s + p_2 Q_2^s$), $y = y(p_1, p_2)$. With the Q_i^s homogeneous of degree zero in p_1 and p_2, it is obvious that y is homogeneous of degree one in the same arguments. Since equations (5.31) are assumed to be homogeneous of degree zero in p_1, p_2, and m, y, and y is homogeneous of degree one in the two prices, it follows that the reduced equations

$$(5.32) \qquad \tilde{Q}_i^d = \tilde{Q}_i^d(p_1, p_2, m)$$
$$\equiv Q_i^d(p_1, p_2, y(p_1, p_2), m), \quad i = 1, 2,$$

are also homogeneous of degree zero in p_1, and p_2, and m. Furthermore, if in equations (5.29) it is assumed that $Q_{ij}^d > 0$, $i = 1, 2; j = 1, 2, y; i \neq j; Q_{ii}^d < 0$, and $Q_{im}^d > 0$; then in equations (5.32) it immediately follows that $\tilde{Q}_{ii}^d < 0$, $\tilde{Q}_{im}^d > 0$, and $\tilde{Q}_{ij}^d > 0, i, j = 1, 2, i \neq j$.

The supply functions (equations (5.30)) can be obtained from the standard neoclassical production functions and some assumptions about the markets for primary factors. Denote supply as

$$(5.33) \qquad Q_i^s = Q^s(K_i, N_i), \quad i = 1, 2$$

where K_i and N_i are the quantities of capital and labor services used in the ith industry. The usual neoclassical assumptions on first and second derivatives are assumed to hold. Now assume that K_i is held fixed in both industries. Then output is a function only of the quantity of labor employed, so that equations (5.33) become

$$(5.33a) \qquad Q_i^s = Q_i^s(N_i), \quad i = 1, 2.$$

The only distinction between equations (5.33) and (5.33a) is that, since the former is homogeneous of degree one in both arguments, the latter is not a homogeneous equation in N_i.

If it is assumed that the total stock of labor is fixed and that demand for labor by each industry is determined by the condition that workers are hired up to the point where the value of labor's marginal product equals the money wage rate, then the labor market can be described by three equations. Two of these give the demand for labor by each of the industries, while the third requires that the total (fixed) stock of labor be fully employed. Therefore,

$$N_1^d = N_1^d(p_1, w)$$
$$(5.34) \qquad N_2^d = N_2^d(p_2, w)$$
$$N_1^d + N_2^d - N = E_N = 0$$

where N_1^d is the quantity of labor demanded by the ith industry, N is the total stock available, and E_N is the excess demand for labor. From the assumption that the money wage rate equals the value of labor's marginal product it follows

167

that each $N_i^d(\cdot)$ is homogeneous of degree zero in w and p_i. At the equilibrium w, p_1, and p_2, labor demand in each industry equals labor supply. Substituting the appropriate labor demand function into the corresponding industry production function, and into the excess demand function yields,

$$(5.35) \qquad Q_i^s = Q_i^s(N_i(w, p_i)) = Q_i^s(w, p_i), \quad i = 1, 2$$

and

$$(5.36) \qquad E_N(w, p_1, p_2) = 0.$$

Equation (5.36), which is homogeneous of degree zero in w, p_1, and p_2, can be solved explicitly for w as a function of the prices. This equation (i.e. $w = w(p_1, p_2)$), which is homogeneous of degree one in p_1, and p_2, can then be substituted into equations (5.35) to give equations (5.30), which are homogeneous of degree zero. Equations (5.30) and (5.32) then immediately yield the excess demand functions of equations (5.6).

This somewhat laborious explanation of the model has two purposes. First, it demonstrates that, since equations (5.6a) can be generated out of a structure where capital is assumed to be industry-specific, any theorem derived in an excess-demand function formulation is equally applicable to worlds of perfectly mobile and perfectly immobile capital. Second, having extensively outlined the basic model, the modifications necessary to convert it to a world of less than full employment can be easily incorporated.

Unemployment in a Walrasian Model

The possibility of involuntary unemployment can be introduced into the model just developed by abandoning the assumption of a fixed stock of labor that must be fully employed and inserting a more Keynesian assumption that there is a contractually fixed money wage rate and an infinitely elastic labor supply curve at that money wage rate. Formally this is done by dropping equation (5.36) (i.e. the third equation in equations (5.34)), and substituting the definition $w = \bar{w}$, where here the bar is used to denote an exogeneously given quantity. (Of course, $w = \bar{w}$ only for $N_1^d + N_2^d < N$.)

This rather simple change has the unfortunate result of destroying the homogeneity properties of the system. Since the full employment requirement has been dropped, the demand for labor by each industry is a function only of the price of the good produced in that industry. Therefore, the supply function for each good has only that good's price as an argument and ceases to be homogeneous. This, in turn, implies that money income is no longer a homogeneous function of the two prices. From this it follows that, although excess demand functions still have the same arguments, they cease to be homogeneous as well.

If the assumption is made that price changes in the industry demand functions can be broken down into Slutsky income and substitution effects, as in individual demand equations, then even without the homogeneity assumption, in a closed economy or in a small open economy with balanced trade, if all goods are gross substitutes, income can be solved out of the model, and the signs of the derivatives of the excess demand functions remain determinate. Specifically, in the two-good model, if

$$(5.37) \qquad E_i = Q_i^d(p_1, p_2, y(p_1, p_2), m) - Q_i^s(p_i)$$
$$= \tilde{E}_i(p_1, p_2, m), \quad i = 1, 2,$$

and if $Q_{ii} < 0$, $Q_{ij} > 0$, $i, j, = 1, 2, i \neq j$, $Q_{im} > 0$, and $0 < Q_{iy} < 1$, $i = 1, 2$, then $\tilde{E}_{ii} < 0$, $\tilde{E}_{ij} > 0$, and $\tilde{E}_{im} > 0$, $i = 1, 2$.

Differentiating equation (5.37) with respect to p_i yields[16]

$$(5.38) \qquad E_{ii} = Q_{ii}^d + Q_{iy}^d \frac{\partial y}{\partial p_i} - Q_{ii}^s.$$

---

[16] Tildes over the E_i have been dropped to simplify notation.

However, Q_{ii}^d can be decomposed into a pure substitution effect, δ_{ii}, and an income effect, $Q_i^d Q_{iy}^d$. Likewise, $\partial y/\partial p_i = Q_i^s + Q_{ii}^s$, so that equation (5.36) becomes

$$(5.39) \qquad E_{ii} = \delta_{ii} - Q_i^d Q_{iy}^d + (Q_i^s + Q_{ii}^s)Q_{iy}^d - Q_{ii}^s.$$

If the economy is closed, $Q_i^d = Q_i^s$ for all i. If it is small and trade is balanced, the same is true for the composite traded good. Therefore it follows that

$$(5.40) \qquad E_{ii} = \delta_{ii} + Q_{ii}^s(Q_{iy}^d - 1).$$

As long as $\delta_{ii} < 0$, $E_{ii} < 0$. A similar argument with p_j yields

$$(5.41) \qquad E_{ij} = \delta_{ij} + Q_{ij}^s Q_{iy}^d,$$

and equation (5.38) is positive if $\delta_{ij} > 0$. Finally,

$$(5.42) \qquad E_{im} = \frac{\partial E_i}{\partial Q_i^d} Q_{im}^d > 0.$$

In the excess demand for money equation it is trivial to establish that, if $\partial m^d/\partial p_1$, $\partial m^d/\partial p_2$, and $\partial m^d/\partial y > 0$, then

$$(5.43) \qquad \tilde{E}_m = m^d(p_1, p_2, y(p_1, p_2), m) - m = \tilde{E}_m(p_1, p_2, m)$$

and $\tilde{E}_{m1}$ and $\tilde{E}_{m2} > 0$, while $\tilde{E}_{mm} < 0$.

The Balance of Trade and Financial Controls

The above discussion implies that the small-country model with a nontraded good and money can be expressed as

$$(5.44) \qquad \begin{aligned} B + p_1\tilde{E}_1(p_1, p_2, m) &= 0 \\ \tilde{E}_2(p_1, p_2, m) &= 0 \\ \tilde{E}_m - \tilde{E}_m(p_1, p_2, m) &= 0, \end{aligned}$$

where good 1 is the composite traded good and good 2 is the home good, and, therefore, $p_1 = ep_1^*$. If equations (5.44) are

170

totally differentiated, and use is made of the assumption that trade is initially balanced, so that $E_1 = 0$, then

$$(5.45) \quad \begin{bmatrix} E_{12} & 0 & 1 \\ E_{22} & 0 & 0 \\ E_{m2} & 1 & 0 \end{bmatrix} \begin{bmatrix} dp_2 \\ dE_m \\ dB \end{bmatrix}$$
$$= - \begin{bmatrix} E_{11} & mE_{1m} \\ E_{21} & mE_{2m} \\ -E_{m1} & -mE_{mm} \end{bmatrix} \begin{bmatrix} de/e \\ dm/m \end{bmatrix}.$$

However, since the equations of the system lack any homogeneity properties, no further reduction or transformation of equations (5.45) is possible. Thus, in general it will not be true that $dB/(de/e) = dB/(dm/m)$. Furthermore, solving explicitly for dB/de yields

$$(5.46) \quad \frac{dB}{de} = \frac{1}{E_{22}} [E_{12}E_{21} - E_{22}E_{11}],$$

and again, without homogeneity properties it will not in general be true that $E_{22}E_{11} > E_{12}E_{21}$. Therefore, the gross substitutability of goods and money is insufficient to insure that a devaluation will improve the balance of trade even without a second financial asset. Moreover, while it is still true that $dp_2/p_2 = -E_{21}/E_{22} \, de \gtreqless 0$, so that a devaluation raises the price of the home good, it is not clear whether or not $dp_2/p_2 \gtreqless de/e$. Thus, several results found in the literature break down when unemployment is allowed in the model. Of course, it is not surprising that different assumptions yield different results. However, the relevant issue in this context seems to be the sort of model desirable in policy applications. In general, Krueger's point is well taken, and a model that requires continual full employment would appear to be much less useful in this connection, regardless of its value as a logical tool.

171

III MACROECONOMIC VERSUS WALRASIAN MODELS:
A SUMMARY

As is immediately obvious from an examination of equations (5.45), even when unemployment is introduced into the model, the assumptions of gross substitutability between commodities and positive marginal propensities to spend are sufficient to guarantee that an increase in the money supply will reduce a trade surplus or increase a deficit. That is,

$$(5.47) \qquad \frac{dB}{dm} = \frac{m}{E_{22}} (E_{2m}E_{12} - E_{1m}E_{11}) < 0.$$

Thus, regardless of whether or not a devaluation improves the trade balance, given these assumptions, the system will be stable in the long run, and the long-run behavior of the Walrasian system with unemployment and money will be essentially the same as that of the Keynesian model described in Chapter 4. Since the similarities and differences between a Walrasian system with bonds and the Classical version of the macro model developed in Chapters 3 and 4 already have been discussed, it is reasonable to ask at this point whether or not there is any reason to prefer one framework over another.

In general, the answer would seem to depend on the purposes for which the model is utilized. At an operational level, there is little formal difference in the two systems. For certain questions—an analysis of the role of nontraded goods, for example—a Walrasian setting seems more useful in that its excess-demand function formulation reduces the problem to more manageable proportions. For other purposes—analyzing the impact of control variable changes on the level of output and employment, say—the more traditional macroeconomic framework seems more convenient. Also, the macroeconomic framework has the advantage of being more readily adapted to an aggregate-expenditure function type of analysis, which at least has the value of permitting a more ready comparison of new results with previous work in the literature.

Beyond the operational level, however, remains the question of the appropriate conceptual framework for monetary analysis. If, as is argued by Clower and others, it is agreed that the logical structure of the Walrasian model precludes a meaningful role for money, then any monetary result obtained in this framework is suspect. In this regard, both the Keynesian macroeconomic framework employed in Chapters 3 and 4, as well as more simplified versions used in other studies in the literature, have the advantage of being independent of the assumption that a Walrasian barter model underlies the "real" portion of the model. In this regard, at least, a macroeconomic framework would appear to be superior to the Walrasian. Of course, the question remains whether or not such models accurately reflect the economics of Keynes, but this is another issue, and beyond the scope of this study.

CHAPTER 6

Conclusions and Disclaimers

THE initial motivation for this study was a belief that one of the main reasons the existing literature had failed adequately to reconcile the conflicting approaches to balance of payments analysis was that the basic research strategy adopted generally was faulty. Rather than begin by setting up a complete open-economy model then use this to analyze payments issues, the more common approach seemed to be to apply a variety of very limited ad hoc models to the problem. As was indicated in Chapter 1, this generated more dispute and discussion than definitive results, and meant that a fundamental issue—the reconciliation of the elasticities and absorption approaches to payments analysis—went unresolved for twenty years.

Circumvention of this apparent impasse in the literature, it was argued, required a more careful specification of an open-economy model than hitherto had been done. The specification and use of such a model was one of the main objectives of this study. The usefulness of the exercise is borne out by the results obtained in the preceding four chapters.

Chapter 2 showed conclusively that the traditional method of extending macroeconomic models to deal with trade problems is inadequate. This inadequacy stems from three factors. The first is that many existing extensions, by virtue of their failure to take account of the problem of defining real variables in an open economy, are seriously misspecified. As Chapter 2 proved, this misspecification implies that significant effects of exchange rate changes on such things as real income and the real value of the money supply are overlooked or omitted. Since these omitted effects are a key part in the successful reconciliation of the relative price and income approaches to devaluation analysis, in retrospect it is not surprising that, with these effects consistently ignored, more progress was not made toward a synthesis.

The second omission in the existing literature was the exclusion of a production, or supply, sector in aggregate open-economy models. Without such a sector, it is difficult at best to permit prices to vary in the devaluing country. This, in turn, was probably at least partially responsible for the failure of many authors to include a terms of trade effect in their analysis, or for such statements as Tsiang's assertion that the Alexander-Harberger two-stage analysis was either logically invalid or extremely restrictive.

After identifying the problems in existing models, a complete macroeconomic model including a production and a monetary sector, and with real variables properly defined, was set out and explained in Chapter 3. This model was then used to analyze the short-run response of output, employment, and the balance of payments to changes in the exchange rate. Insofar as output and employment are concerned, it was shown that (1) in a case with Keynesian unemployment, a devaluation might lower the level of employment and output even if it suceeded in generating an improvement in the net balance of trade; and (2) in a Classical full-employment case a devaluation would always lower the level of output and employment. For the balance of payments, completely general expressions for the effect of a devaluation on the trade balance in both the Keynesian and Classical cases were obtained. As might have been expected, in as complete a model as was employed here, these effects were quite complex. However, it was shown that results found in earlier contributions in the literature could be obtained as special cases of these complex general results. Furthermore, these results supported the contention in Chapter 1 that Tsiang's criticism of the two-stage synthesis procedure was unjustified.

As might have been expected, in the Keynesian version of the model, when price, income, and monetary variables are incorporated, the famous Marshall-Lerner condition is neither necessary nor sufficient to insure that a devaluation will improve the balance of trade in the short run, although it does appear in the final expression. However, it was also shown that, if the Marshall-Lerner condition is met, the overall sufficient condition for a devaluation to improve the trade balance in the short run is made less stringent. Less expected, however, was the result, also shown in Chapter 3, that in the Classical version of the macro model (with an aggregate expenditure function), the Marshall-Lerner condition was a sufficient (but not necessary) condition to insure that a devaluation would improve the balance of trade.[1] It was noted that this last result was in direct contrast to the findings reported in the monetarist literature, where a devaluation always leads to a short-run improvement in the trade balance.

In Chapter 4, the long-run impact of a devaluation on the economy was examined. In this chapter it was shown that, without complete sterilization of the monetary effects of a trade surplus or deficit, the Keynesian model behaved in essentially the same fashion as the Hume price-specie-flow model, as first reported by Mundell. However, it was shown that, for this result to hold, long-run stability of the model had to be guaranteed. In Chapter 4, it was shown that a sufficient set of conditions to guarantee this long-run stability was that all goods be gross substitutes and that the Marshall-Lerner condition hold. In the Classical model, the same conditions were shown to be necessary to insure stability.

If the long-run stability conditions are met, in the Keynesian

---

[1] In addition, a stability analysis of the model was provided. In this analysis it was shown (1) that there is no single stability condition when the Correspondence Principle is used, and (2) that under any reasonable adjustment structure, the model could reasonably be assumed to imply stable behavior.

case, a devaluation raised the level of output and employment, although it had no long-run impact on the balance of trade, while in a Classical world neither employment and output nor the balance of trade were permanently affected by a devaluation. While in one sense this reconfirmed results found in various monetarist analyses, it also showed that, contrary to monetarist findings, the result was not automatic, but rather required that the Marshall-Lerner condition be met in order to hold.

Chapter 4 also examined the role of monetary and fiscal policy in the short and long runs. It was found that, in the short run, a result first reported by Hahn and subsequently reconfirmed in monetarist studies—that equiproportional devaluation and decreases in the home money supply in a Walrasian model have equal effects on the trade balance— holds in the Classical version of the macroeconomic model as well. However, this result did not carry through in the Keynesian model due to the lack of homogeneity introduced by the fixed money wage rate. In the long run, as long as the system is stable, it was shown that monetary policy was completely ineffective in both the Keynesian and Classical systems. When fiscal policy was examined, it was found that, although effective in the short run, expansionary expenditure policies could be completely ineffective in the longer term, even in a Keynesian environment, unless the government followed a "buy domestic" policy.

In both Chapters 3 and 4, the model used was developed without the real balance effect incorporated into the behavioral equations. Since in Chapter 3 it was shown that the elasticities and absorption approaches could be completely integrated without such an effect, while other monetarist results were obtained as special cases of the analysis conducted in Chapter 4, it seems fair to conclude that the real balance effect does not warrant the attention given it in the monetarist literature. As the analysis of Chapters 3 and 4 suggests, the real issue in payments analysis is the nature of the production sector assumed to exist, and, in particular, whether or not continuous full employment is assumed.

Chapter 5 turned to an examination of the Walras-Hahn approach to payments analysis. Since Chapter 4 had found that some of the results obtained in this framework carried over to the Classical macroeconomic world, it was felt that a closer examination of the relationships between the two methods of analysis was in order.

The mechanism at work generating the Hahn-Kemp result necessarily was the real balance effect, whereas in the macroeconomic model an interest rate effect alone was sufficient to generate the result. When bonds and a rate of interest were introduced into the Walras-Hahn framework, the result no longer held. Moreover, the Hahn, Kemp, et al. proposition that devaluation improved the balance of trade if all goods and money were gross substitutes failed to carry through to a world with bonds. However, with a slight modification, Kemp's theorem that a two-good model with money can be interpreted as a three-good model with money so long as one good is nontraded carried through to a world with both money and bonds. However, the Kemp-Krueger-Dornbush result—that the relative price of the home good unambiguously falls with a devaluation—thus inducing a decline in the production of home goods and an increase in the output of traded goods—failed to carry over when bonds were added to the model.

Since these results were obtained in the standard Walrasian framework of fixed factor supplies and full employment, the model was modified to allow for a variable labor supply and unemployment. In this case, the model behaved much as did the Keynesian version of the macroeconomic model discussed in Chapters 3 and 4, and none of the theorems found in the Walrasian literature on devaluation analysis went through. It was argued that, although this was the result of varying the basic assumptions used by Hahn, Kemp, Krueger, Dornbush, and others, the real issue was which set of assumptions was more useful for policy purposes.

Although this is a fairly sizable list of new results, much remains to be done. In particular, in a departure from recent trends in the literature, this study has ignored the capital account, and focused exclusively on the trade account. Obviously, this is an unrealistic simplification. The main justification for this omission is that it permitted a sharper focus on the basic structure of the model developed here. This, in turn, made it easier to demonstrate that, in fact, the three approaches to devaluation analysis—elasticities, absorption, and monetarist—were in fact successfully synthesized and reconciled in this study. Moreover, as was argued in Chapter 4, properly to incorporate capital flows would require an explicitly dynamic, rather than comparative static, analysis.

Finally, the world described here is one of perfect certainty, or else very naive expectations. Since international economic affairs are perhaps the least certain of any aspect of economics, it is obvious that work should be done to relax this assumption.

REFERENCES

Aghevli, B. B., and G. H. Borts (1973), "The Stability and Equilibrium of the Balance of Payments under a Fixed Exchange Rate," *Journal of International Economics, 3* (February 1973), 1–20.

Alexander, S. S. (1952), "Effects of a Devaluation on the Trade Balance," *International Monetary Fund Staff Papers, 2* (April 1952), 263–278. Reprinted in Caves and Johnson.

—— (1959), "Effects of a Devaluation: A Simplified Synthesis of Elasticities and Absorption Approaches," *American Economic Review, 49* (March 1959), 23–42.

Allen, P. R. (1973), "A Portfolio Approach to International Capital Flows," *Journal of International Economics, 3* (May 1973), 135–160.

Barro, J., and H. Grossman (1971), "A General Disequilibrium Model of Income and Employment," *American Economic Review, 61* (March 1971), 82–93

Berglas, E., and A. Razin (1972), "A Note on 'The Balance of Payments and Terms of Trade in Relation to Financial Controls,'" *Review of Economic Studies, 39* (October 1972), 511–513.

—— (1973), "Real Exchange Rate and Devaluation," *Journal of International Economics, 3* (May 1973),

Branson, W. H. (1968), *Financial Capital Flows in the U.S. Balance of Payments*, Amsterdam: North Holland Publishing Co., 1968.

—— (1970), "Monetary Policy and the New View of International Capital Movements," *Brookings Papers on Economic Activity*, Vol. 2

—— (1972), *Macroeconomic Theory and Policy*, New York: Harper and Row, 1972.

Brems, H. (1957), "Devaluation, A Marriage of the Elasticity and the Absorption Approaches," *Economic Journal, 67* (March 1957), 49–64.

Brownlee, O. H. (1950), "The Theory of Employment and Stabilization Policy," *Journal of Political Economy, 58* (October 1950), 412–424.

Caves, R. E., and H. G. Johnson, eds. (1968), *Readings in International Economics*, Homewood, Illinois: Richard D. Irwin, Inc., 1968.

Clement, M. O., R. L. Pfister, and K. J. Rothwell (1967), *Theoretical Issues in International Economics*, Boston: Houghton Mifflin Company, 1967.

REFERENCES

Clower, R. (1965), "The Keynesian Counterrevolution: A Theoretical Appraisal," in F. H. Hahn and F. P. R. Brechling, eds. *The Theory of Interest Rates,* London: Macmillan and Co., Ltd., 1965.
―――― (1967), "A Reconsideration of the Microeconomic Foundations of Monetary Theory," *Western Economic Journal, 6* (March 1967), 1–9.
Dornbush, R. (1971), "Notes on Growth and the Balance of Payments," *Canadian Journal of Economics, 4* (August 1971), 388–395
―――― (1973a), "Currency Depreciation, Hoarding and Relative Prices," *Journal of Political Economy, 81* (July–August 1973), 893–915
―――― (1973b), "Devaluation, Money and Nontraded Goods," *American Economic Review, 63* (December 1973), 871–880
Ellis, H. S., and L. A. Metzler, eds. (1950), *Readings in the Theory of International Trade,* Homewood, Illinois: Richard D. Irwin, Inc., 1950
Flanders, M. J. (1963), "The Balance of Payments Adjustment Mechanism: Some Problems in Model Building," *Kyklos, Fasc. 3, 16* (1963), 369–380
Frenkel, J. A. (1971), "A Theory of Money, Trade and the Balance of Payments in a Model of Accumulation," *Journal of International Economics, 1* (May 1971), 159–187
―――― and C. A. Rodriguez (1975), "Portfolio Equilibrium and the Balance of Payments: A Monetary Approach," *American Economic Review, 65* (September 1975), 674–688.
Hahn, F. (1959), "The Balance of Payments in a Monetary Economy," *Review of Economic Studies, 26* (February 1959), 110–125.
―――― (1965), "On Some Problems of Proving the Existence of an Equilibrium in a Monetary Economy," in F. H. Hahn and F. P. R. Brechling, eds. *The Theory of Interest Rates,* London: Macmillan and Co., Ltd., 1965.
Harberger, A. C. (1950), "Currency Depreciation, Income and the Balance of Trade," *Journal of Political Economy, 58* (February 1950), 47–60. Reprinted in Caves and Johnson.
Herschliefer, J. (1973), "Exchange Theory: The Missing Chapter," *Western Economic Journal, 11* (June 1973), 330–336.
Johnson, H. G. (1956), "The Transfer Problem and Exchange Stability," *Journal of Political Economy, 64* (June 1956), 212–225.
―――― (1958), "Towards a General Theory of the Balance of Payments," in his *International Trade and Economic Growth,* London:

182

REFERENCES

Irwin University Books, 1958. Reprinted in Caves and Johnson.
—— (1967), *Essays In Monetary Economics*, Cambridge: Harvard University Press, 1967.
—— (1972), "The Monetary Approach to Balance of Payments Theory," *Journal of Financial and Quantitative Analysis, 7* (March 1972), 1555–1572.
Jones, R. W. (1961), "Stability Condition in International Trade: A General Equilibrium Analysis," *International Economic Review, 2* (May 1961), 199–209.
Kemp, M. C. (1962), "The Rate of Exchange, the Terms of Trade and the Balance of Payments in Fully Employed Economies," *International Economic Review, 3* (September 1962), 314–327. Reprinted in *The Pure Theory of International Trade and Investment* as Chapter 14.
—— (1969), *The Pure Theory of International Trade and Investment*, Englewood Cliffs, N.J.: Prentice-Hall, Inc., 1969.
—— (1970), "The Balance of Payments and the Terms of Trade in Relation to Financial Controls," *Review of Economic Studies, 37* (January 1970), 25–31.
Keynes, J. M. (1964), *The General Theory of Employment, Interest, and Money*, Chicago: Harcourt, Brace and World, Inc., 1964.
Komiya, R. (1967), "Non-Traded Goods and the Pure Theory of International Trade," *International Economic Review, 8* (June 1967), 132–152.
—— (1969), "Economic Growth and the Balance of Payments," *Journal of Political Economy, 77* (February 1969), 35–48.
Krueger, A. O. (1965), "The Impact of Alternative Government Policies under Varying Exchange Systems," *Quarterly Journal of Economics, 79* (May 1965), 195–208
—— (1969), "Balance of Payments Theory," *Journal of Economic Literature, 7* (March 1969), 1–26.
—— (1974), "The Role of Home Goods and Money in Exchange Rate Adjustments," in W. Sellekaerts, ed. *International Trade and Finance: Essays in Honour of Jan Tinbergen*, White Plains, New York: International Arts and Sciences Press, Inc., 1974.
Laursen, S., and L. Metzler (1950), "Flexible Exchange Rates and the Theory of Employment," *Review of Economics and Statistics, 32* (November 1950), 281–299.
Leijonhufvud, A. (1968), *Keynesian Economics and the Economics of Keynes*, New York: Oxford University Press, 1968.

REFERENCES

Machlup, F. (1955), "Relative Prices and Aggregate Spending in the Analysis of Devaluation," *American Economic Review*, 45 (June 1955), 255–278.

—— (1956), "The Terms-of-Trade Effects of Devaluation upon Real Income and the Balance of Trade," *Kyklos*, Fasc. 3, 9 (1956), 417–450.

Markowitz, H. (1959), *Portfolio Selection: Efficient Diversification of Investments*, New York: John Wiley and Sons, 1959.

Marschak, J. (1951), *Income, Employment and the Price Level*, Chicago: University of Chicago Press, 1951.

McKinnon, R. I. (1969), "Portfolio Balance and International Payments Adjustment," in R. A. Mundell and A. K. Swoboda, eds. *Monetary Problems of the International Economy*, Chicago: University of Chicago Press, 1969.

—— and W. E. Oates (1966), "The Implications of International Economic Integration for Monetary, Fiscal and Exchange Rate Policy," *Princeton Studies in International Finance*, No. 16, Princeton, N.J.: Princeton University Press, 1972.

Meade, J. E. (1951), *The Balance of Payments: Mathematical Supplement*, London: Oxford University Press, 1951.

Metzler, L. A. (1948), "The Theory of International Trade," in H. S. Ellis, ed. *A Survey of Contemporary Economics*, Vol. I, Homewood, Illinois: Richard D. Irwin, 1948.

Michaely, M. (1960), "Relative-Prices and Income-Absorption Approaches to Devaluation: A Partial Reconciliation," *American Economic Review*, 50 (March 1960), 144–147.

Mundell, R. A. (1961), "Flexible Exchange Rates and Employment Policy," *Canadian Journal of Economics*, 27 (November 1961), 509–517.

—— (1968), *International Economics*, New York: The Macmillan Company, 1968.

Negishi, T. (1968), "Approaches to the Analysis of Devaluation," *International Economic Review*, 9 (June 1968), 218–227.

Patinkin, D. (1965), *Money, Interest, and Prices*, New York: Harper and Row, 1965.

Pearce, I. F. (1961), "The Problem of the Balance of Payments," *International Economic Review*, 2 (January 1961), 1–28.

—— (1962), "Community Consumer Demand Theory," *Australian Economic Papers*, 1 (September 1962), 1–23.

REFERENCES

Purvis, D. (1972), "More on Growth and the Balance of Payments," *Canadian Journal of Economics*, 5 (November 1972), 531–540

Richardson, J. D. (1971), *Devaluation and the Terms of Trade*, Reprint QM 7103, Social Systems Research Institute, University of Wisconsin, March 1971.

———— and R. M. Stern (mimeo), "An IS-LM Exposition of Policies for Internal and External Balance," Unpublished Manuscript.

Robinson, J. (1937), "The Foreign Exchange," in her *Essays in the Theory of Employment*, Oxford: Oxford University Press, 1937. Reprinted in Ellis and Metzler.

Samuelson, R. A. (1965), *Foundations of Economic Analysis*, New York: Atheneum, 1965.

———— (1966), "A Summing Up," *Quarterly Journal of Economics*, 80 (November 1966), 568–583.

Sohmen, E. (1957), "Demand Elasticities and the Foreign Exchange Market," *Journal of Political Economy*, 65 (October 1957), 431–436.

Takayama, A. (1969), "The Effects of Fiscal and Monetary Policies under Fixed and Flexible Exchange Rates," *Canadian Journal of Economics*, 2 (May 1969), 190–209.

———— (mimeo), "Stability Conditions, Comparative Statics and the Correspondence Principle in an Open Economy," Unpublished Manuscript.

Tinbergen, J. (1941), "Unstable and Indifferent Equilibria in Economic Systems," *Revue de l'Institut International de Statistique*, 1941.

Tobin, J. (1965), "The Theory of Portfolio Selection," in F. H. Hahn and F. P. R. Brechling, eds. *The Theory of Interest Rates*, London: Macmillan and Co., Ltd., 1965.

Tsiang, S. C. (1961), "The Role of Money in Trade-Balance Stability: Synthesis of the Elasticity and Absorption Approaches," *American Economic Review*, 51 (December 1961), 912–936. Reprinted in Caves and Johnson.

Vanek, J. (1962), *International Trade: Theory and Economic Policy*, Homewood, Illinois: Richard D. Irwin, 1962.

Yeager, L. B. (1970), "Absorption and Elasticity: A Fuller Reconciliation," *Economica*, 37 (February 1970), 68–77.

Irving Fisher Award Series

1. Richard Roll, *The Behavior of Interest Rates: The Application of the Efficient Market Model to U.S. Treasury Bills*, New York: Basic Books, 1970.
2. Charles R. Nelson, *The Term Structure of Interest Rates*, New York: Basic Books, 1972.
3. Michael Szenberg, *The Economics of the Israeli Diamond Industry*, New York: Basic Books, 1973.

Library of Congress Cataloging in Publication Data

Kyle, John F   1943–
  The balance of payments in a monetary economy.

  (Irving Fisher award series)
  Based on the author's thesis, University of Wisconsin.
  Bibliograph: p. 181
  Includes index.
  1. Balance of payments—Mathematical models.
2. Macroeconomics—Mathematical models. I.   Title.
II. Series.
HG3881.K94   382.1'7   75–15280
ISBN 0–691–04208–X

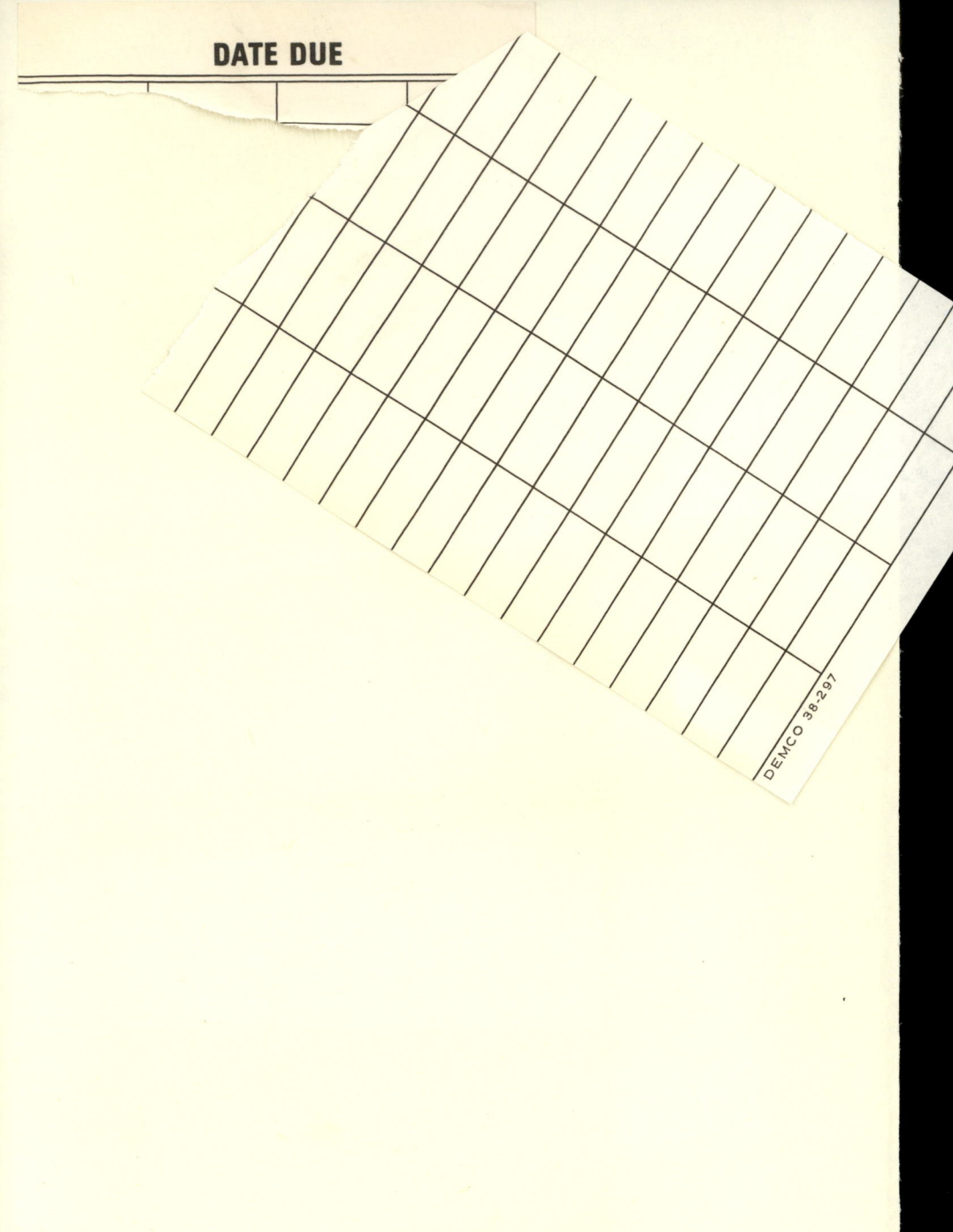